Seeds of Violence

Seeds of Violence

*The Autobiography of a
Subversive*

B.J. Mitchell

To order additional copies of this book, contact:
Xlibris Corporation
1-888-795-4274
www.Xlibris.com
Orders@Xlibris.com
29895

This book is dedicated to my mother, who protected me to the best of her ability even while she was in danger herself. She taught me to care about others who are less fortunate than I, and to live the way God expects us to live. It is also dedicated to my Godparents, Aunty and Uncle, who were totally honest and ethical and who treated everyone, including each other, with respect. Finally, this is dedicated to my little, crippled grandmother who was forever positive in spite of her constant pain. She taught me to love the simple things of life.

The lower levels of hell are reserved for those who in times of moral crisis remain silent.

—Dante Alighieri

CHAPTER 1

It was one of those lazy afternoons in late autumn when the air is warm and still. In the distance the mournful wail of a train could be heard, a long blast of sound, then quiet; another long blast of sound, then quiet. A baby was lying on a blanket under a big oak tree, gurgling happily and rolling from side to side.

As the train grew closer, the baby began to roll off the blanket and down a steep embankment toward the railroad tracks. As she hit the tracks, a five-year old boy was running toward her, sensing the horror of what was about to occur. The baby was too stunned to cry and the boy was too scared to scream. As the train went roaring by with a long continuous frantic wail, the small boy was dragging the baby up the hill to safety. The engineer had seen the child but there was no possibility that the train could stop in time. I was that child and the young boy was my uncle. That was the beginning of a life of adventure, turmoil, success, and failure. It could have been a violent ending to an unfortunate beginning, but it turned out to be a forecast of difficult times to come. It was definitely my first encounter with potential violence, but certainly not my last.

It was 1931, and the nation was in the depths of an economic depression. Dad (actually my grandfather) was a dirt farmer, scratching a bare existence from poor, rocky Missouri Ozarks land. When my mother, just sixteen years old, became pregnant with me, Dad picked up his family and moved to Iowa. The plan was to leave with eight family members (Dad, Ma, my mother, her four brothers and one sister) and to return with eight family members. I was to remain behind in Iowa at a home for unwed mothers, to be adopted out. No one who knew the family would know about me. In those days it was a mortal sin and a terrible disgrace to have a child without benefit of marriage.

In the wee hours of a spring morning in 1931, my mother gave birth to a four-pound future subversive. No one knew at the time that I would become a subversive, but it was written into my soul. The neighbor who delivered me didn't have the assistance of a doctor's skilled hands, nor painkillers, nor any other benefits of modern medicine. I was delivered at home, in a place that was unfamiliar to my family, to a seventeen-year-old, bewildered country girl with no husband. The odds were definitely not in my favor to become a successful anything, much less a successful subversive. But I was born a Taurus, so the negative odds were tempered by a strong will and an elephant size determination. However, my birth, a result of the violence of rape, was just the beginning for my mother.

My first triumph was being born while my Grandfather (I called him "Dad" because that's what my uncles and aunt called him) was away looking for a home that handled adoptions for unwed mothers who were unable to keep their children. But I was having none of it—this was the home I had picked to be born into and here I was going to stay. So despite my unimpressive size, I slipped into my Grandmother's loving arms and stole her heart. Once Ma held me the die was cast and she refused to let me be given away. Some would call that simply "fate," but I call it carefully planned destiny. More about that later.

Iowa was only a temporary stopover for my family and me. Six months after I was born, we were back in the Missouri Ozarks where we belonged-nine of us this time: me, my mother, Dad & Ma, my four uncles and one aunt. This had to have been a terribly difficult time for my poor mother. In those days it was rare for a young girl to give birth without benefit of marriage, and the ones who did were definitely not well received into the community. They were considered "bad girls." While that would be extremely difficult for both my mother and me, the strong community disapproval did keep many young girls from having babies casually, unlike the behavior in today's "anything goes" culture. I am not advocating that we return to those days when young girls were treated cruelly, whether or not the mishap was their fault. But it would seem appropriate to at least attempt to stem the tide of fatherless children.

Dad never believed my mother's story that she was raped, and neither did the community. As far as I know, no one in the family talked about it or asked any questions. She told me the sordid details many years later, when I was an adult. It was a totally believable story. But never mind the facts, people looked at her askance; some even told their children they were not to play with me because I was "not the kind of child you should be seen with." It was years before I would understand any of this, but it was indelibly imprinted on my mind. Despite her efforts to protect me from the cruelty of insensitive people, the harshness of reality took its toll on us both.

My first memory of life was of a log cabin deep in the woods where I lived with Dad and Ma, my uncles and aunt. It was incredibly small for that many people. My mother had gone into a nearby town to work as a hotel maid, then a housekeeper, in order to make enough money for the family to survive. Those who are old enough to remember the "Great Depression" will appreciate what a big deal it was just to have a job of any kind. For a teen who had only finished the eighth grade, a housekeeping job was quite respectable. My mother had tried to go to high school, but the only clothes she had to wear were hand-me-downs from an elderly woman for whom she worked. The other kids made so much fun of her "old woman clothes" that she quit school in humiliation. I have never forgiven our snobbish society for not teaching children to respect everyone, including the poor and unfortunate. As you can see, the seeds of subversion were sown very early in my life.

The cabin where we lived had one room, plus an add-on kitchen, and a sleeping loft; that was all there was. There was no electricity and the only running water was in the spring down the hill from the cabin. As soon as I was big enough, I carried a quart bucket (that had once held cooking lard) down to the spring several times each day and filled it with water for cooking and drinking.

My two youngest uncles were only five and eight when I was born, and it was much later that I learned they were my uncles and not my brothers. Their chores included shooting squirrels and rabbits, which were a large part of our diet, and trapping furry animals, like raccoons and foxes, whose pelts could be sold for extra money to buy staples. They also had to work in the field, cutting brush, digging out stumps and clearing off the rocks, so that the land could be used for planting.

My two older uncles and my aunt were away most of the time, working for other people, accepting any job that would pay a few pennies, or a chicken or two if they got lucky. I don't remember my mother ever being there. Probably she was, but I didn't know who she was until much later. If she was there, I never made the connection, and I never *really* knew who she was until after she died and I discovered her diary. But I'm getting ahead of myself.

The cabin was sparsely furnished. In the kitchen there was a wood cook-stove, a small kitchen table and chairs, and an open cabinet of shelves for dishes and pots. The living room had a bed for Dad and Ma, an old wine-colored sofa, a couple of chairs, and a wood stove for heating. A ladder in one corner led up to the sleeping loft, which had straw mattresses on the floor with feather pads on top and hand made quilts. The stovepipe from the wood stove in the living room ran through the loft floor and out the roof, providing a small bit of heat in the winter. Dad had to get up several times during the night to add wood to the fire. Basically, we were just cold all winter.

The outbuildings consisted of a rickety old shed, housing the few farming tools we possessed, and the outhouse—hot in the summer and cold in the winter, and always devastatingly offensive to the nose. Parts of Montgomery Ward and Sears Roebuck catalogs were available for finishing the job, and you quickly learned to look for the pages that were black and white because they were softer. You also learned not to sit down without looking for snakes first. If there is ever another "great depression," we really can all survive without cable TV, video games, cell phones, and Kleenex.

Dad never raised much in the way of crops because the land was so poor, and because he loved to drink and gamble, he often spent the seed money for worldly pleasures. Ma was a sweet, gentle, kind and loving person who never had a harsh word to say about anyone—not even Dad. She welcomed him home with open arms when he went on a binge and spent all the money they had saved for groceries. At the time I was too small to resent it, and anyway Ma always managed to feed us with something like fried squirrel and a vegetable from the garden. Sometimes it was just gravy, made from flour and water, and a biscuit. With enough salt and pepper the gravy wasn't bad. As was the case with most poor Ozarks dirt farmers, we managed to survive.

Ma was the love of my life. She was grotesquely crippled with arthritis in all her joints. Tiny and frail and in constant pain, she shuffled about taking care of the house, the garden, the laundry, the kids, and Dad. I never heard her complain, but sometimes I would see her softly rocking back and forth with tears running down her cheeks from the pain. If she saw me watching, she would wipe her eyes and say, "come on child, let's go out and look for pretty rocks and flowers." And off we would go, to my great delight. I had to be very careful where I stepped because the woods were full of snakes and lizards, not to mention thistle weeds with stickers, and I only had shoes for winter wear. Usually the delight of finding a pretty wildflower, or a rock with a bit of sparkling quartz, was enough to make me forget all about the snakes. To this day, I usually walk with my eyes toward the ground, just in case.

Dad paid little attention to me, (or to Ma either, for that matter) and for that I was grateful for he was often quite cruel to the boys. They were mischievous, as boys tend to be, and if he caught them playing when they were supposed to be working in the field, he would whip them soundly with a small limber branch from a sassafras bush. Sometimes they would sneak off and go to the schoolhouse to try and learn to read and write. If he caught them, they suffered the lesson of the stick. It was scary for a small child to watch. They both grew up to be good men, but you could sometimes see the remnants of the lessons they learned from their father about the way that children were to be treated. Those lessons from early childhood seem to follow us throughout our lives. The discipline of children is a very sensitive and complex issue.

At the time it seemed quite natural that we should create our own toys and games. Everyone did that, because no one had money to do otherwise. Today I am most grateful for that necessity. It developed our skills to be creative, to dream up things that did not exist, to think about why trees don't all look alike, and other interesting aspects of life. In other words, it taught us to think and create. Today's children seem to have so little creative space. Sometimes I think the glare of commerciality, the overwhelming deluge of toys and diversions, is at least as bad as drugs and alcohol. The effect is on the mind rather than on the body, but it is equally devastating.

My uncles made whistles out of slippery elm branches, tall stilts that we could walk on, and wheelies out of a long stick with a tobacco can on the bottom end with the edges turned up forming a U-shaped receptacle. It took little skill to run a lard can lid down the stick, catch it in the tobacco can, and skitter off down the path into the

woods as fast as I could roll it before it ran
faster than I could. We played "mumblypeg"
(a game we played with a pocket knife and
a bulls-eye drawn on the ground) and ate
green gooseberries. We put the fuchsia juice
of polk plant berries on our faces and rode
stick horses as we played cowboys and
Indians. We went blackberry picking so that
Ma could make jelly and her special
blackberry cobbler.

I had no idea that we were desperately poor
because everyone we knew lived pretty much
the same way we did. Even though most of
the local farmers were more responsible than
Dad, they still had to struggle to keep their
heads above water, so to speak. Some had
wells for water, and a few livestock and some
chickens for food, which was more than we
had, but they all had outhouses and no
electricity. The ones who were somewhat
better off gave shoes and clothing that were
outgrown to those of us who were unable to
buy anything for ourselves. People cared
about their neighbors, and they didn't
withhold help because Dad was a ne'er-do-
well. They saw a family in need and they
responded. No one ever suggested that the

family should be punished for the sins of the father.

How did we lose our way? Today we whine and complain that children are growing up without proper parental supervision, while at the same time requiring women without husbands at home to go to work and leave their children in the hands of strangers, many of whom are ill equipped to teach proper values. Some even harm the children emotionally and/or physically.

Many mothers lack the skills to earn salaries large enough to afford proper childcare facilities, but our society doesn't appear to worry about that—it is a common view that we can't allow a mother to live off of tax dollars. After all, why should they be entitled to anything they didn't earn? What we can do (and do) is whine and complain that their children are not receiving proper training. Unfortunately, women who grow up in a violent home environment need training themselves in order not to repeat the violence with their own children. The seeds of violence are sown very early in a child's life. Research has shown that witnessing domestic violence as a child is the most common risk for becoming a batterer.

The same tragedy happens to women who know they can't afford to raise a child properly and want to abort the fetus during the first trimester. Many in our government, made up largely of affluent males, insist that the mother carry the baby to term while at the same time refusing any responsibility for the proper support of the child into adulthood. That makes no sense to me. It is just another way of saying that women have no rights. Personally, I believe that if the government ever denies the woman's right to make her own decision about abortion, then the government should take responsibility for paying for the child's living expenses and education until that child is eighteen years old. That is only fair.

The rocky land where our little log cabin sat yielded adequate vegetables to be canned for winter. There was no money for fertilizer so there could be no prize-winning tomatoes or melons, but the garden was sufficient to provide food for the winter. There was an apple tree and a peach tree, so we had canned applesauce and peaches from the cellar for pie in winter. Only about five acres had been cleared, with the rest of the surrounding area being forest, mostly consisting of post oak, black walnut, elm, sassafras, and other species. There was an occasional persimmon tree for the pleasure of the 'possums. The fruit also made good pie, but it was generally too much trouble to climb the tree to get the persimmons so, for the most part, they were left to the critters.

Of all the animals we ate from the woods, the least palatable was the 'possum. I only remember one time that we were left with nothing else to eat but a mean looking 'possum. Even when you are very hungry it is hard to swallow. It has a very strong wild flavor, and is heavily endowed with fat. It was dreadful! Probably we should have roasted him over an open fire and stuffed him with persimmons. I liked the squirrel with dumplings and the fried rabbit, but may God deliver me from any more 'possum.

As I write this I find myself smiling. The food that seemed perfectly good at the time now sounds like a horror movie when it is described in print. But I was actually better off in the long run from my diet as a child. There were no candies, no rich sauces, no soda pop, no prepared foods saturated with chemicals, no potato chips, and very little pastry. On rare occasions we would be invited to a nearby farm for homemade ice cream, but that was truly rare. Once in awhile Ma would bake sugar cookies, but that was also rare—sugar and flour were too costly.

With all the inconveniences, I can truthfully say that this was probably the happiest time of my life. I had absolutely no sense of the depth of our poverty. I had enough to eat, fun games to play, shoes in the winter, and a loving granny to talk to. She taught me how to watch out for the things that might harm me, and told me funny stories about her own childhood. I can't remember any of them, but I remember being happy and content. Someone gave me a book when I was about three, and Ma read it to me so many times that I memorized it all. When company came to visit I would "read" it to them—I even knew exactly when to turn the page. I don't know if Ma ever told them that I really couldn't read, that I had just memorized it. But from that moment, I was hooked on books.

Sometimes Dad worked at a sawmill in another community. I don't think he brought much of the money home, however, because nothing ever seemed to change there—no new furniture or clothes or sweet treats. Ma made all our clothes from flour sacks. Most of the companies that sold flour made the sacks in different patterns so that the poor would have material to use for clothing. No one in our neck of the woods had any money for buying fancy cloth, and I think it was pretty much that way all around the country. Some of the sacks came in plain white and that is where our underwear came from. Sometimes the people my aunt worked for would send an item of clothing home for one of the family. There was a lot of "handing down" in those days.

There were no churches anywhere near our area. Sometimes a preacher would hold a revival meeting in the schoolhouse a few miles away. Occasionally we would build a "brush arbor" in the woods and a "traveling preacher" would hold services there. We sat on logs in this open-air cathedral—just a roof made of pieces of small bushes. The preachers were of various faiths so I was exposed to a wide range of religious thought.

I remember one preacher was from a denomination that believed in foot washing. He brought pans of water and we all washed each other's feet. I thought it was a bit embarrassing because my feet were always pretty grungy, given that I had no shoes for summer. But I sat through it bravely, as did everyone else. Looking back I can see that this kind of exposure was a positive rather than a negative. It saved me from the narrowness of a single set of religious dogma. I learned about right and wrong from Ma, and later from my mother. What they said rang true, so I had no problem with it.

Our cabin was seven miles from the nearest road, so strangers didn't just wander by. We didn't care that there were no roads nearby, because no one we knew had a car. We didn't have a horse either, so if we went anywhere it was on foot.

Of course I was too young to go anywhere alone, so I stayed close to my uncles. One day when I was about three years old they took off through the woods and told me that I couldn't go. Unfortunately, they expected that I would do as I was told, so they never looked back. I followed them deep into the woods until I couldn't keep up any longer, then I realized that I was lost. The trees around me all looked like giant monsters instead of the friends they had always been to me, and there was no path that led to home. I began to cry, but there was no one to hear. The fear was overwhelming; I was panic-stricken.

I wandered around in the woods for hours until I finally came upon a house. I remember a nice couple feeding me cake and trying to find out who I was and where I came from. I had no idea. I had not been exposed to strangers much, so I ate my cake without saying a word. After what seemed like an eternity, my uncles showed up to find me. When they had returned to the cabin and I was not there, they too had panicked, knowing that they were supposed to be watching me and instead had allowed me to wander off. After that they were careful to be sure I was in the house when they went off, so that I couldn't follow them.

I still love the woods and I love to hike, but I don't like to go anywhere there is not a path so I can find my way back. The denseness of the forest where I was lost gave me a feeling of being closed in—the suffocating thicket of trees and the feeling of panic seem to go together, and it causes me to avoid large crowds, heavy traffic, elevators, and small rooms without windows. Today, my home is on a mountain with the front windows open to a huge expanse of open space. I can see for fifty miles. The forest I love is behind me, with a road running past it.

Clearly, being lost in the woods was one of those "defining moments" that psychologists love to babble about. Despite the residual fear of that experience, I still feel most at home when I am in the woods. I don't like cities and I am ill at ease in the desert. I'm not sure where the discomfort in the desert comes from—perhaps simply the absence of trees.

The lessons learned from this period of my life are these: (1) being poor is okay, unless someone tells you it isn't—only then do we begin to feel sorry for ourselves. And by poor I mean that you have adequate food, clothing and shelter, a means of transportation, and the necessary medical attention, but nothing beyond basic needs. This just may be the most ideal of lifestyles: adequate but sparse, with no toys to keep the family from talking and playing together, and no long hours at the office just to buy the toys that keep families from talking and playing together. Beyond that, money can be a liability rather than an asset.

(2) We are all in the same boat when it comes to surviving on this planet. We all need to paddle hard to keep the storms from upsetting the boat, and we all need to paddle together. We should not throw someone overboard because he isn't paddling as hard as the rest of us, and we certainly shouldn't throw his family overboard because he isn't paddling fast enough. We need to teach him how to paddle more effectively, and it wouldn't hurt us to teach him why it is important to paddle at all. Perhaps most

important, we might try teaching his children why they should not emulate his behavior when they grow up.

This part of my life came to an end one warm summer day (I couldn't have been more than four years old) when Dad carried me through the woods to a little country store and post office, and put me in the back of an old pickup truck that carried the mail to a small town some fifty miles away. This was the town where my mother worked as a housekeeper for an ex-Congressman and his wife. I had no idea where I was going, and I was too scared to ask. The back of the truck where I rode alone, with mailbags and packages, was closed in, hot, and dark. Images of being lost in the woods swirled around me.

The bumpy, stop-and-go, jerk and lurch ride seemed endless. The makeshift seat was uncomfortable, and periodic stops when the driver had to get into the back where I sat to get packages for the people along the delivery route, raised my fears that I would be dumped off somewhere where strangers would whisk me away to an unknown fate.

This scary routine was repeated many times during the trip, which was probably not more than two or three hours long—but a very long time for a small child to sit still, stuffed into the corner of a bumpy truck.

When the truck stopped at the town's post office, I was taken out of the truck with the other packages and taken inside. I had never seen a town, and as small as it was it seemed huge, noisy, and scary. At four years old, I was sure that my life was over. Who and what would greet me at the end of my trip (if indeed it were ever to end) would shock and dismay me for what was to seem to this small, skinny, bewildered child like an eternity.

CHAPTER 2

The stranger who picked me up at the post office was a pretty lady, dark brown hair, blue eyes and, like all adults, very large. In truth, she was only five feet two, but bigger than Ma so that made her a giant to me. She said simply, "I'm your mother; you're going to live with me now." She picked up the flour sack with my clothes and my book and led me outside to a car where a tall man with grey hair was behind the steering wheel. I sat in the back seat alone, my heart pounding, wondering what these two were going to do with me. I had not spoken a word since I was deposited unceremoniously into the mail truck.

The man in the front seat tried to talk to me, but I was having none of it. My mother tried to talk to me too, but I was having none of that either. I was exhausted, I needed to go to the outhouse, and I just wanted to be back in the woods with Ma. I watched the houses zipping by (in those days the fastest anyone ever drove was 30 mph), and then rolling countryside with, thankfully, some trees.

Finally, we arrived at a long driveway leading to a big brown, two story farmhouse. A sweet looking lady, no bigger than Ma, was waiting for us at the door. She gave me a big smile and picked me up in her arms. She peppered me with questions about the trip. I remained silent. "You can call me Aunty," she said, "and this is Uncle;" she pointed to the man who had driven the car.

The kitchen was huge, as big as our whole house in the woods. A big wood stove sat in one corner and a very large table with many chairs around it was in an alcove just off the kitchen. I had never seen anything remotely like this. Our table at home was made from unpainted boards and the chairs were simple cane bottom hand made seats. This table was polished wood and so were the chairs—with fancy cloth on the seats.

In one corner of the kitchen Aunty had put a small child's chair. "This is your chair," she said. "You can sit on it and watch your mother cook wonderful things to eat. If you are good, she might let you sample some." She smiled at me and squeezed my hand. I sat down and watched my mother make lunch.

My mother didn't talk much. Occasionally she would look at me and ask if I wanted anything. Finally, unable to hold my bladder any longer I said, "I need to go to the outhouse." Imagine my surprise to find that the outhouse was inside the same house we lived in. That was the beginning of a long series of surprises. I slept upstairs with my mother in a soft bed, in a warm room.

It didn't take long for me to learn that Aunty and Uncle were kind, gentle, loving people— like Ma. There was no one in the house to fear. No one got whipped for doing the wrong thing. My mother didn't talk much, she was too busy cooking, cleaning, doing laundry, and other things that go along with keeping house. Aunty took care of me. She took me shopping and bought me clothes, took me to the doctor when I needed it, and always read the funnies to me on Sunday morning before church.

Life was now very different for me. After a long period during which I could not eat the food because it was too rich, I began to like my new life. Aunty fussed and worried because I wouldn't eat (I was terribly skinny anyway) and eventually figured out that my system was just unable to digest the pot roast and gravy, green beans seasoned with bacon, and mashed potatoes swimming in butter. She fixed a special plate of simple, unseasoned food for me and gradually added regular food to my diet until I could tolerate the food they ate. She squeezed fresh orange juice to try and make me healthier and, when I wouldn't drink it because it had pulp in it, she carefully strained out all the pulp. She fed me cod liver oil to make me stronger. I told her that Ma never did anything awful like that to me, and I kicked and screamed when the bottle came out. Finally, that job was delegated to my mother.

Eventually I would learn that Aunty and Uncle were wealthy people by the standards of that day. The depression was still in full bloom, and many people were still scratching for enough money to buy food and pay the rent. I, on the other hand, was living quite well. Uncle had been a congressman for one term. He couldn't stand the politics of Washington,DC, so he never ran for re-election. I treasure the scrapbook, with pictures and party invitations from that period in their lives, which Aunty gave me before she died. She didn't like the Washington DC life either, however. They chose to return to their Missouri roots where Uncle became a Circuit Judge.

My memories of that period of my life are warm and peaceful. Uncle would take Aunty and me with him on his rounds to other towns where he was holding court. We would go shopping while he worked—he would never let us attend the court proceedings because, he said, "Court is not a proper place for nice ladies and little girls." I regret deeply that I never had a chance to see him perform his duties as a judge. I know he was a good one because he was much loved and respected everywhere he went.

I don't remember doing much with my mother. She was always busy taking care of the house and garden. Some evenings she

would get dressed up and leave with a tall
thin man in an old beat up car. They would
be gone until long after I had gone to bed.
Aunty would read to me and play games with
me—we became quite close; she really had
nothing to divert her attention from me.
Sometimes I missed Ma and our walks in the
woods, but mostly I just enjoyed being
pampered.

This time in my life is somewhat fuzzy in my
memory. I remember getting just about
everything I wanted. One day I was shopping
with Aunty and Uncle in a small town where
he was holding court, and I found a
kaleidoscope that I really wanted. Aunty
thought she had bought me enough for one
day and so declined to buy it. I was
heartbroken and I'm sure I must have shed
a few tears along the way. The day after we
returned home Uncle gave me the coveted
kaleidoscope because he couldn't stand to
see me so disappointed. He had gone back
to the store and bought it before we left
town. He didn't want to go against Aunty's
decision in front of me, but he hated to see
me cry. That same day, the mailman
delivered a second copy that the store

manager had sent. I'm sure he didn't care a whit about what I wanted, but Uncle was a very important figure in the town so he wanted to make a few points. In any case, I usually got what I wanted.

This happy period in my life was brief, not more than a couple of years. One day my mother introduced me to the tall thin man saying, "This is your stepfather. We are married and you and I are going to live with him on his farm." I was not happy. It wasn't as scary as the ride in the mail truck, but it was just as uncomfortable. It was not a happy time for me. It wasn't happy for Aunty either. My mother told me later that Aunty and Uncle wanted to adopt me; they had no children of their own. She had declined because "you would have grown up with too much money and never have amounted to anything on your own." She was probably right. However, I think she may have regretted that decision later.

What I learned from this chapter in my life was that happiness does not depend on whether you are rich or poor. It depends on how much love you experience. When I was first poor, I had great love for Ma and she for me. When I first lived in a wealthy household I had great love for Aunty and Uncle and they for me. I eventually learned to love my mother, but I never learned to even like Pop, much less to love him. It certainly wasn't because we were poor; it was because he did not give love nor did he want it. He got a great deal of it from my mother, but if he loved her back he had a funny way of showing it.

CHAPTER 3

Moving to the farm was like being dropped into a tub of ice water. When we finally arrived, my step-grandmother was waiting for us. The farm was hers and my stepfather had stayed behind to work the family farm when his siblings moved on to lives of their own. She was definitely not warm and fuzzy. And she definitely did not like my mother and me moving into her domain.

Pop (I finally learned to call my stepfather something other than "sir") was her "baby" and she treated him like one. He didn't like to get up early, so she would keep his breakfast in the warming oven above the stove until he was ready to eat. No one in the house could sit down at the dinner table until he was in his place, and no one dared to sit in his place. He had a special plate and cup that no one else dared to use. She didn't like my mother in her kitchen, but she also didn't like having to cook for four either. She

never tried to hide her feelings from either
of us.

My mother tried to make the best of a
miserable life, and I just tried to stay quiet
and out of sight. There was no Ma and no
Aunty to pay attention to me. I felt very, very
alone. My mother was a very good mother,
but she had her hands full just trying to keep
a semblance of married life and trying to
keep the dissension in the house to a dull
roar. Of course, it didn't help that there was
no indoor plumbing and the bathroom was
an outhouse again. Trudging through the
snow in the middle of the night was no
picnic, and that was the least of my
discomforts. For me, life had gone from
happy, to happy, to miserable.

Aunty mailed the funnies to me every week.
I couldn't read yet but I enjoyed looking at
the pictures and it kept me connected to her
in some small way. My resident "grammaw"
belonged to a religion that didn't believe in
gifts or Christmas trees or radios or anything
that was fun. So we didn't celebrate birthdays,
or Christmas, and God forbid we should look
for the Easter Bunny. As fate would have it,

grammaw died a couple of years later and the three of us were alone on the farm.

One might logically assume that things got better for my mother and me. But one would be wrong. Without grammaw there to keep order, Pop made no effort to hide his drinking. I soon learned that he had been a closet abusive alcoholic. Now, with his mama gone, he was just an abusive alcoholic. The seeds of violence were taking root.

Without Aunty to keep me busy, I was back to entertaining myself. Much of the time I helped my mother in the kitchen and in the garden. Pulling weeds from the vegetables or washing jars for canning, carrying in wood for the stoves, feeding the chickens. Sometimes I helped Pop in the fields. I had to clear the fields of rocks and sometimes I thinned the rows of corn in the fields. In those days when you planted corn, the planter wasn't always accurate and it would drop more than one seed in a hill (the corn hills were about a foot apart). After the corn was up, I would follow the rows and pull out the extra stalks of corn. That made the ears on the surviving stalk much larger. I guess that makes sense; at the time it didn't. My back always hurt from bending over for long periods, but I learned to live with it and not to complain openly.

And always there were the cows to milk. I had three of the less cantankerous cows that were my responsibility. Each morning, bright and early while the frost was still on the grass, I trudged off to the barnyard where the three bovines awaited me. "Be careful she doesn't kick over the bucket," or "don't let her get her tail in the milk." My mother was full of instructions because she didn't want Pop to be angry with me, which he surely would have been if I had lost any of the milk.

By the time I was eight years old I was driving the tractor to haul loads of grain to the threshing machine. It was a big, red Farmall and it was very scary. I was still quite small for my age and I could barely reach the pedals from the edge of the seat. I was always afraid that my foot would slip and the tractor would be out of control, or that I would drive too close to the men who were throwing bundles of grain on the wagon and hurt someone. The only redeeming quality of this

job was that I didn't have to help with the
dishes after lunch.

I breathed a sigh of relief when September
came and it was time to go back to school. I
didn't particularly like school, but it was
better than washing jars and driving the
tractor. I walked the mile of country road to
attend classes, through rain, snow, heat, or
whatever weather presented itself. In the
spring there were gooseberries and wild
hazelnuts growing in the fencerows along the
way, and that relieved the boredom of the
long walk. I was quite small for my age,
which was a lucky break because the boys
didn't beat up on me. There was always one
of the bigger boys who protected me.

It was a small country school, one room with
all eight grades together. The teachers were
all pretty good despite the fact that most did
not have teaching degrees. We were far from
any town, with little money for salaries, so
we didn't exactly attract the top of the line.
Nonetheless, I learned to read and write and
diagram a sentence, and I was forced to
memorize the multiplication and division
tables. I have always been grateful for this,

not because it was fun but because the teacher hammered us until we could recite them all by memory. That is a skill I have used to good advantage all my life. How sad it is that today kids only have calculators. Often I find it important to be able to calculate something quickly in my head. Without those demanding teachers, I wouldn't be able to do that.

At home what I learned most was fear. Pop would go through periodic drunken binges, which often turned into drunken rages. My mother would send me upstairs to bed where I would soon be awakened by loud voices and banging and crashing. I was scared nearly out of my wits. What if he killed her? What would I do if I had to live with him alone? I could hear her cry and I couldn't do anything about it. Eventually I would lie awake, heart pounding, and listen for the noise to begin. One day I saw him kick her off the porch, which was probably two feet off the ground. After that, I could barely tolerate him.

I spoke very little when he was drinking, afraid of making him angry. I learned to be

aware of what might set him off and to avoid
those subjects. It was like walking on
eggshells. Sometimes I would beg her to take
us both somewhere else to live. But she
would say, "He is a good man—it's my fault
when he gets mad—I say things I shouldn't
sometimes—it's all my fault—you must never,
ever, tell a soul about this." Now I
understand that this was just typical "battered
woman" behavior. At that time I didn't
understand any of it, but I never told a soul.

For six years I struggled against the fear and
tried to pretend I liked this man whom I
not only feared, but disliked intensely.
Clearly, my mother loved him and I tried
hard not to make her life more difficult
than it already was. As a child I never
understood how she could care for a man
who treated her so badly. I never understood
it until after she died and I read her diary.
Then it became clear. But I'm getting
ahead of myself again.

One night when I was twelve years old, there
was a particularly loud banging and crashing
downstairs. It went on for a long time as I
held my breath, fearing for my mother's life

as well as my own. Finally, my mother came to the bottom of the stairs and yelled at me, "Go get Jim (he was our closest neighbor about a quarter of a mile down the road) and tell him to come quick—he's trying to kill me—Hurry!!"

I put on my overalls and boots and got my coat and ran down the stairs. My mother was standing in her underwear while Pop lunged at her—he had already torn off her clothes. He missed her, then grabbed the poker and swung at my head as I ran by him and out the door. Fortunately, he missed me too. He swung the poker so hard that he turned all the way around and fell to the floor; that let me escape out the door.

The race to the neighbor's house is a nightmare that haunts me to this day. It felt like I was running in slow motion. It was like my feet had big weights attached to them— I could barely pick them up and I knew I had to hurry.

When I finally arrived at the neighbor's house, Jim wouldn't come to help. "I'm not going to get into a couple's fight—this is between the two of them." I sat down and wept. What would I do now? It was miles to the next farm, she could be dead before I got there. And what if he wouldn't come either? The pit of my stomach was jello. What would I do without her? What could I do to save her? Should I go back and try to help? But if I did go back, what could I do? I knew that would simply mean my mother would have both of us to try to protect instead of only herself. I could do nothing.

Within half an hour my mother showed up at the neighbor's house. She was dressed only in her slip and she spoke through the screen door to Jim's wife, asking if she would lend her something to wear. She handed out a robe and my mother came inside. Of course she was greatly embarrassed— domestic fights were never aired in public. She had managed to get the car keys from Pop so she gathered me up and we left. She drove us to Pop's brother's home and we stayed there overnight. They didn't get along very well with Pop, and they didn't like my mother and me, so they just made my mother feel worse by having to admit she had been beaten up again.

The next morning we went home. I begged her not to, but she said, "He won't hurt us now—he will be sober now and he will be really sorry for what he did." I wasn't so sure. I was still suffering from the shock of the previous night and I was scared to death of him. When we arrived he was still asleep and we came in quietly to assess the damage. The kitchen looked like a cyclone had passed through. Pop had broken every dish in the house against the walls; glass jars of vegetables were broken in the middle of the floor; he had taken a bottle of bluing and thrown it all over the walls. Literally everything was dragged out of the cabinets and thrown around the kitchen.

My mother began cleaning up the mess, and I helped. I wanted to tell someone, to ask for help, but I didn't dare. Many years later, when I had become a full time writer, I was finally able to talk about it. It was too late to prevent my lifelong fear of the dark, of sudden noises, of intimidating people.

It is this troubling period of my childhood that causes me today to try and do something to change the attitudes of the general public toward domestic violence, indeed against all violence.

In California we have a law that requires ANYONE working with children to report to the police any suspicion of child abuse. This is a good thing, but it does not help the millions of kids who live in abusive homes but do not bear visible evidence of the abuse—kids who are damaged emotionally but who would never tell anyone about it. They are no better off than I was, with no one to turn to for help—no one to tell them that it is not their fault—no one to share the pain and fear.

It was after that awful night that my mother realized I was in danger and that she had to do something about it. I'm sure it never occurred to her that she was in danger too, and that she should remove both of us from the source of danger. I didn't understand that until later either. Her solution was to move me back into town with Aunty and Uncle. That was the greatest gift she could have given me.

CHAPTER 4

It was a year before I could sleep through the night without being awakened by every innocent sound. When Uncle went to the bathroom I would sit bolt upright in a panic, sure that Pop was at it again. A clap of thunder, a sudden rainstorm, any noise at night would awaken me. But the rest of my life with them was idyllic. It could not have been more different from the previous six years.

Aunty and Uncle were unlike any couple I have ever known, before or since. They respected each other, they enjoyed the same things: classical music, theatre, fine literature, helping those less fortunate. In the six years I lived with them, before I went away to college, I never once heard a cross word between them. They would sit in front of the fireplace and discuss practical and political issues: what was happening in the community, editorials in the *St. Louis Globe Democrat,*

Aunty's bridge game. Their disagreements
were always respectful.

That has been my role model for all of my
adult life. Only once did I encounter a
"situation" between the two of them. Uncle
was a deacon in the Baptist Church and
Aunty was a Methodist. In those days the
wife was expected to go with her husband to
church, regardless of what her own
preference might be. One Sunday the Baptist
preacher prayed for the Catholics and the
Methodists, that they might see the error of
their ways and be saved from eternal
damnation. In the car on the way home,
there was an awkward silence. Finally, Aunty
said, "Well, I really don't think it was
necessary for him to pray for the Methodists."
Uncle said nothing and the subject was
closed. I never heard it mentioned again.

I have always wondered what made them
different from the rest of the world. How
could we teach that to young couples before
they get married? Is it even possible to teach
civility and respect? On the other hand, why
couldn't it be taught? Why couldn't schools
be required to teach mandatory ethics and

debating skills classes? Discussion and debate are healthy and necessary for a good relationship; yelling at each other is not. It is particularly bad for children; they are likely to be insecure anyway and listening to parents fighting adds to that insecurity. Anyway, my godparents were wonderful role models and I would wish that for all children. Unfortunately, we are a long way from that.

At the time I didn't realize it, but living with Aunty and Uncle gave me many advantages later in life. In the little town where I went to school, there was a social chasm between the "townies" and the kids from the country who were bussed in. Since Aunty and Uncle were at the top of the social hierarchy, their status was automatically transferred to me. As a result, I was given every opportunity to participate in any activity I wanted, to be elected to office in school clubs, in short, to learn leadership skills.

These are all confidence-building exercises. You learn how to speak before groups and to lead a group toward a particular goal. It definitely gives you a leg up when you start to pursue a career because you already know how to make yourself seen and heard. And perhaps most important, you learn how to get others to help you accomplish what you want to get done.

Fortunately, I never forgot my country roots. It was important to me to let the country kids know that I knew we were all equal. And I was well aware, even as a teenager, that social status is never a predictor of personal worth. I was the same person who had once been "the wrong kind of child to play with," and I never forgot that my new exalted status was none of my own doing. Anyway, my godparents were people of great personal worth and they would have been the same with or without money and prestige. My mother was also a person of great personal worth even though she had neither money nor prestige. This is one reason I am a big supporter of uniforms for all school children. It levels the playing field so that no one knows who has money and prestige and who doesn't.

There are many things our communities need to help children find their way in a complex world. For example, every community should have a club that is open to all children, without regard to family income or social status, who are willing to live by a particular set of rules. *The Secret of Hilhouse*, by P.J Pokeberry, tells of "The Ribbit Society" which is just such a club. Ribbit Society rules are simply rules that make a human being more civilized such as:

> Never take an action that is harmful to yourself or someone else;
>
> Keep your mind clear, active, and always learning;
>
> Keep your body at its healthiest possible level;
>
> Never do something just because everyone else does it;
>
> When in doubt, ask your soul for direction.

Unfortunately, most children grow up thinking that "some pigs are more equal than others," and they show it by gathering in little cliques to the exclusion of others who don't "measure up." I always hated that because I knew that if not for Aunty and Uncle, I would have been one of the less equal pigs. Part of teaching children to be civilized is helping them understand that in God's eyes we are all equal. Much of the violence committed by children against their own peers is psychological, but no less damaging.

What is really sad is that the children who find themselves on the outside, look for acceptance in the wrong places—the one group that welcomes anyone and everyone with open arms is the group that uses drugs and alcohol. In a recent television interview where I was discussing *The Secret of Hilhouse* and the Ribbit Society, a young man called in to the show to tell me that. He said, "All of us want to belong to a group, but the elite groups won't accept just anyone so we turn to the druggies—they will welcome anyone who is willing to take drugs. Once you are hooked, you can't get out."

That still haunts me today. Why can't we understand that and make a warm, welcome place for kids who need a place to belong? You are probably thinking that this is the

church's place. I would respond that the
church is a good place, but the members are
primarily adults. The children need a club that
is all theirs—a club just for kids, a club that
requires no particular religious belief. Also,
children who are left out of the clubs are often
those who have no church affiliation.

Anyway, I took advantage of my newly
acquired status and participated in everything
I could: band and orchestra, choir, debate,
school plays, anything that looked
interesting. I was never turned down for
anything I wanted to do. Aunty encouraged
me to participate and she always made sure
that I had whatever I needed to do so. She
even kept a scrapbook of everything I did,
every office I held, every event I played or
sang in. Years later I was surprised by some
of the things in that scrapbook. I had
forgotten many of the joys and triumphs of
my teen years.

In return for all they gave me, I tried to give
them something back. I worked hard to
make sure my behavior never embarrassed
them or worried them. It wasn't always easy
because there were times when I just wanted

to follow the crowd down whatever path they chose. Drink a little booze, smoke a cigarette (in those days these were big events—today they are just part of the expected), go to a party past curfew. Why not? I guess I declined because respect begets respect. Aunty and Uncle respected me and in turn I respected them.

Don't get me wrong. When I say they respected me I don't mean they let me do everything I wanted. They set reasonable limits and I observed them. I told Aunty things that I was thinking and doing. She listened and discussed them with me. It seems so simple, but it must not be. If it were, it would be happening today on a broad scale. It isn't. In today's world, many mothers work and that probably works against the kind of relationship I had with Aunty. Also, some parents think they should be friends with their children; they shun setting limits so there is little for which discipline can appropriately be administered.

Then one day my simple, carefree life was over. It was time to graduate from high school and move into the adult world. I thought I wanted to be a newspaper reporter, so Uncle proposed sending me to Columbia University in New York, because he considered that to be the best journalism school in the country. But I had never been to a big city, had never been anywhere larger than my small hometown of 1,500. I was too shy and too insecure to go that far from home. Instead, I went to a small state college just 100 miles from my home. As it turned out that was a wise choice, for my academic background left a great deal to be desired. Even at the small college I chose, I was deficit in math and science and just about everything else. Although I had been Salutatorian of my high school class, my first year of college was a struggle.

The lesson I learned during this period was simple: it usually matters what kind of parents you have. How well you succeed as a youngster often depends on how much love and support you have at home. It depends on how well respected your parents are by the community and what kinds of values they exhibit. I'm sure there are exceptions to this, as there are exceptions to most cause/effect situations. But there is no doubt that parents play a huge role in the success or failure of their children in school as well as in social settings. I often wonder why all communities and schools do not offer parenting classes. Parenting is the most important and difficult job any adult can have. We take lessons to learn how to drive a car; if we wreck the car we can get a new one. We have no lessons to teach us how to be good parents; if we wreck the child, he/she is often wrecked for life.

CHAPTER 5

Some of the useful things I learned in college were how to pour tea and make appropriate small talk with the public, and how to wear high heels, hats and gloves. In those days, young ladies dressed up to go to parties—we even wore hats and gloves to go shopping in the city. When I stop to think about it, I wonder why we did all those strange things. I guess it was because we behaved in a more civilized way when we were dressed more formally, or at least we thought so. I joined a sorority and my sorority sisters quickly taught me social skills. That gave me a sense of belonging and eliminated most of my insecurities. They also taught me some of my less useful skills like smoking and beer drinking. I never let beer parties interfere with my studies, but I certainly never found college dull, either.

There were two major interests in my college life, besides sorority activities: earth sciences and the young man I stood behind in the college choir. I quickly fell in love with the back of his head. He had just been dumped by his girl friend, who immediately married the other guy, so he was quite vulnerable to my flirtatious ways. I won his heart—at least temporarily. I still had a year of school left when he graduated, and we were married three days before he left for the Air Force. The Korean war was in full swing at that time and young men were being drafted immediately upon graduation from college. I saw him one time during my last year in college; I visited him for a week during Christmas vacation.

With my major distraction off to war, I buckled down and studied hard. Although my major was sociology, I loved my classes in earth sciences: physical and historical geology in particular, but also climatology, meteorology, and geomorphology. One other girl ventured into a class or two, but most of the time I was the only girl in the class, because young women had not yet been told that they were smart enough to take classes in the sciences. Aunty and Uncle had always told me that I could be anything I wanted to be if I were willing to work hard enough, so I didn't need the approval of society as a whole. I think that was the beginning of my determination to think my own thoughts and be my own person.

That stubborn mindset has guided me all of my adult life. I am unashamed to be viewed as a political liberal (not all liberals enjoy that freedom), I am perfectly happy being close to God without being connected to a church (although I might feel comfortable in one that does not pray for the Catholics, or any other religious group, to mend their ways), and I feel free to disagree with absolutely anyone regardless of income or social status. I am quite comfortable in my own skin.

That last year of college was actually a fun year. My husband's younger brother had just begun his college career at the same school where I attended, and he escorted me to all the parties and important events. We had a grand time. I was crowned sorority sweetheart that year, and that was the highlight of my college days. It was a particularly sweet triumph for a shy farm girl from the Ozarks. As soon as I graduated, I was off to join my husband at Lackland Air Base in Texas. But it was too late. My husband and I were literally strangers. I knew his brother better than I knew him. I had gone from a carefree, fun life to a life of money woes and responsibilities instead of fun.

Within a few weeks after my arrival, my husband went into Officer Candidate School and was not allowed to come home for six months. After three months we were able to visit on weekends, but the distance between us grew. I looked for work as a social worker, but I was quickly informed that in Texas they only hired graduates of Texas colleges. No out-of-staters need apply. Finally, I found a job as Head Cashier in the Menger Hotel in San Antonio, and by the time we were able to actually live together, we had little in common. We also had little time to develop anything in common. The violence of war often damages relationships through long separations.

We were soon transferred to Cheyenne, Wyoming, then to Wichita Falls, Texas, then back to Missouri where my husband had a teaching job. I got a job as a social worker, but found myself surrounded by other social workers who did not have college degrees, and who made life pretty miserable for me. I lasted two weeks. Then I worked in an office as a cost accountant while my husband became a very popular teacher. We worked at our marriage for 12 years, but the gap between us never closed. He was busy; I was lonely. He was involved in little theatre; I studied art. He wanted me to stay at home and raise a family; I wanted a career of my own.

Eventually, he took a teaching job in Kansas City and I worked as supervisor of accounts receivable for a company that manufactured Meals-on-Wheels. I studied art at the Kansas City Art Institute; we both drank too much. Finally, he returned to his original teaching job and I stayed in Kansas City to sell our house. One morning I got up to go to work, opened a beer instead of fixing coffee and toast, and knew I was in trouble. I couldn't stop crying. A friend came and read poetry to me and stayed with me until he was sure I wasn't going to do myself in.

Clearly, I was on the verge of a nervous breakdown. My friend called my husband

and told him I was in major trouble and needed his help, but he was too busy to come. I knew then that I had to make a change, and that I had to get as far away from my current surroundings as possible. California was as far away as I could go without a passport.

But I couldn't bring myself to go, to give up on a marriage that I knew in my heart could not work. I pooled my money with a fellow artist and we set out to open an art shop in the old mansion my husband had rented for us in a town a few miles from his school. We sold both our cars and bought a VW camper for transporting art objects. She had connections with several professors and students at the university where she had studied art, and several of them agreed to let us take some of their paintings on consignment. In the meantime, my husband was supposed to get the city permits for a variance to allow us to open an art shop in the home we lived in, which was not zoned for business.

The house was truly magnificent. It was located in an area of huge, turn of the

century homes, a remnant of the days when
that town was rich from mining successes.
This one had three floors and a huge wine
cellar, six bedrooms and three baths, a
magnificent spiral staircase with crystal
chandeliers that were as big as some
bathrooms I have known. The gallery was
to encompass the entire first floor, with living
quarters on the two upper floors. But alas, it
was not to be. The local city fathers did not
want an art gallery in their old, but still quite
fancy, neighborhood, and refused to grant
the permit.

As we were packing the paintings to return
to their owners, my friend said to me, "When
are you going to face reality? This marriage
cannot survive. It is time for you to build a
life for yourself, in a career that you will be
happy in. I'm heading for California—why
don't you come along?" The lump in my
throat was as big as an apple. I wanted to
go, but I didn't want to go. I felt very much
like I did at eighteen when I considered
attending Columbia University. I would be
leaving everything I knew, everyone I loved,
my dearest friends with whom I would sit on
their floor, drink tea or wine, and discuss the

philosophy of Ayn Rand, among others. And, of course, my husband whom I loved but could never seem to reach (and with whom I had little in common), would be out of my life forever. It was the most completely unsettling and fearful time of my life.

Finally, I gritted my teeth and stepped out into the unknown, with a handful of clothes and $100 in my pocket. My friend had kept in touch with an old college chum who lived in Los Angeles, and she was kind enough to take us in until we could find jobs. It was scary, but eventually we both managed to find work. In the meantime, we lived on nickels and dimes; at one point the three of us lived for a solid week on a pot of spaghetti and meat sauce. And now I had to decide what to do with the rest of my life.

After failing as a social worker, I decided that I wanted to be a librarian, so I set about to find a school I could afford to attend. I first tried UCLA, but they rejected me because of my age; I was 36 and their age limit was 35. I tried USC, and they also had an age limit of 35. I managed to convince the Dean that I was just barely past 35 and that I should be accepted because I was so close to the qualifying age.

She finally gave in and I scurried to the financial aid office to get a loan for tuition. He looked at me and shook his head. "There is no possible way you can live on the amount of money you have." I pleaded, got teary eyed, and convinced him that I had friends who had promised to help me. Reluctantly, he gave me the loan and a small grant, and with a little help from my friends, I survived that year on 35-cent Banquet TV Dinners.

It is hard to summarize in a few paragraphs exactly what I learned during this period of my life. I pondered for a very long time the differences between my husband and me. Primarily, I concluded, the difference related to our backgrounds, our early childhood. Never being sure how long I would be staying in any particular place, I was a person who needed a close, secure relationship. I needed constant reassurance. At the same time, he had come from a secure, loving family and needed very little from anyone else, including me.

It is my opinion that many couples suffer from this chasm. We tend to give to our mate what we want to get back from them. So a needy person will give the self secure partner more love than they need or want, and the self secure partner, feeling smothered, will pull away leaving the needy partner to feel even more insecure. If couples were to discuss their levels of need with each other, I think more marriages would survive.

I like to compare relationships with empty wine bottles. As children, our parents fill one third of the bottle with love and affection, then our close friends fill another third with acceptance and support, and our partner fills the last third with love and devotion. If my bottle isn't two thirds full when I marry, then my partner is going to have to give me more than a third to fill my bottle. Some partners are prepared to do that (the ones who also have bottles that are less than two thirds full), and some are not. In my case, my bottle had a sufficient amount of love in it, but little security. For the person whose bottle is completely empty, it will be an uphill battle for both the person with the empty bottle and the partner, no matter what is in the partner's bottle.

I guess I also learned that the "happily ever after" story is sometimes just a fairy tale. The lesson for girls is this: never marry until you have some kind of skill with which to support yourself. I have heard young girls say things like, "Oh, I don't need to go to college—I just want to get married and raise a family." I cringe. Yes, they have a slightly less than 50/ 50 chance of a successful marriage, but those are not very good odds. And I recently read a statistic that the divorce rate is higher for "born again" Christians than for the general population, so don't think you can beat the odds by marrying someone from your church.

Whomever you choose to marry, your chances of a permanent relationship are still less than 50/50. It is akin to that famous Ronald Reagan slogan, "Trust but verify." In this case it would be, "Trust but be prepared." Being prepared to support yourself lets you stay in a marriage because you want to and not because you have to. That will help prevent you from making too many demands on your partner for constant reassurance.

Perhaps most important, if you end up in an abusive relationship, you won't be forced to stay in it. You may think that taking advice about marriage from someone who failed at it is not too smart. I believe that we are exactly the ones who can give advice on what not to do. In my case, I was not in an abusive relationship, but I did grow up in one so I feel free to offer advice. It is important to understand that the seeds of violence are everywhere, often under the surface where they are not immediately identified. It requires a willingness to see reality in all of its aspects, good and bad, in order to know when a relationship is about to become abusive.

CHAPTER 6

By the time I finished my graduate degree at USC, I had landed a job at California State University, Northridge as an acquisitions librarian. I made $5,000 a year, and I was sure I had died and gone to heaven. This was a major turning point in my life. I loved my work; I loved the wonderful world of books, and I loved the academic environment. It was my graduate work and subsequent years as an administrator at CSUN that developed my love of research. I found myself being interested in all kinds of things. The days were not long enough to read about everything I was interested in.

Unfortunately, because of my past experience in accounting and supervision I wound up in administration instead of reference. However, that turned out to be a good thing in the long term. I ended up in a position that is now the Associate Dean of Libraries (before librarians achieved faculty status it

was titled Associate Director) and as a result
was in a position to make a real contribution
to the profession. Because of yearly budget
cutbacks by the State, my staff was constantly
asked to do more with less until I finally said
"enough!" I developed a cost analysis
program to tie staffing formulas to services
provided and wrote two books detailing the
program. They were published by an eastern
academic press as part of their *Library and
Information Science* series. They had a wide
distribution, both in the US and overseas,
and even today you will find them listed in
the catalogs of many university libraries. One
of the books was used as a library textbook
at USC.

My love of research, and my curiosity about
all things spiritual, eventually led me away
from management theories and down a
philosophical path to the creation of some
tools for living that I thought might bring
some measure of inner peace. I was
particularly interested in the growing number
of people for whom violence was (and is) a
way of life. Was there some way to bring
those people into a communication with
their soul? If that turned out to be possible,

would it lead them away from a life of violence? It occurred to me that many of them do not believe in God and/or the soul, and that any effort to foster soul communication would have to begin with a rational explanation of what God is. Many people are not able to accept, on pure faith, that God is real simply because someone says they should. I felt strongly that any description of God that non-believers could accept must have some scientific basis—especially those prone to violence. This began a long and interesting research journey.

It was during this time period that I met an interesting group of people who were friends and colleagues of an authentic psychic. This was another important crossroads in my life. The psychic was married to a scientist and the two of them were looking for connections between the spiritual and the scientific. They were wonderful, ethical people, and I began to be fascinated with the idea that God and the scientific world might be one and the same. I had long pondered the question of who/what God is, and the time had come for me to decide what I really believed about God.

I understand that this is a question that can never be answered with any certainty, but I am a person who needs to know what I believe and why. My scientist friend said in one of his lectures, "If you want to know more about God, you should learn about particles and waves." I didn't have a clue what he was talking about, but I began to read books about particle physics to try and find out. Most of it was over my head, because physics was not one of the subjects I had studied in my travels through academia.

Little by little I began to form a picture of God and an explanation that satisfied me about what God might be. I concluded that since everything in the universe is made up of particles and waves (photons, protons and electrons), each particle must be programmed to perform the function that it is designed to perform. That would mean that each performs the same function at every moment in time so that the universe behaves in an organized and predictable way. This vast collection of particles, I decided, must be the mind of God. That would certainly support the view of God as

SEEDS OF VIOLENCE 69

omniscient, omnipotent, and omnipresent (a holdover from my Baptist upbringing). Can this theory be tested in a laboratory? I hope that some dedicated physicist will try. My own role was to put together a string of logic using the bits and pieces of books I have read and many hours/months/years of thinking.

My idea of a true philosophy is one that has no contradictory parts, so I began to try my view of God on various other parts of my belief system. For example, if God controls the programming, does that mean that I have no control over anything that happens to me? That would make me a fatalist, and somehow that did not sound right. Why would God have created humans if they were not to have some role in their own destiny? Eventually I concluded that humans were created with free will choice, which would mean that God does not interfere with the decisions they make. If I get drunk and kill someone with my car, that is not God's will, it is my own.

So why were we given free will choice in the first place? That was a tough one for me to deal with because we have so terribly abused

that power. Finally I concluded that we are
intended to use our free will choice to create
beauty in the world and perhaps, eventually,
even in other parts of the universe. We are
free to either love or hate God, or to reject
the whole idea of God; it is our choice. After
all, love cannot be forced; it must be
voluntary. To love God is to *be loving* and to
create beauty; to hate God is to be hateful
and create ugliness. You cannot love God and
create ugliness, and you cannot hate God
and create beauty.

It is easy to identify by their actions those
who love God and those who hate God. It is
not so easy to identify those who just reject
the existence of God, because some of those
people create beauty and some create
ugliness. To reject the idea entirely that God
is real is to deny the existence of some very
strong scientific evidence that the universe
is the result of a grand design, which suggests
a grand designer. Here are some examples.

An informative book by Paul Davies (winner
of the million dollar Templeton prize for
progress in religion in 1995) titled *God and
the New Physics,* finds the most compelling

evidence for a grand design to be what scientists call the "fundamental constants of nature," that is, certain quantities that have the same numerical value everywhere in the universe and at all moments in time. For example, an atom of hydrogen in a distant star has the same size, mass and internal electrical charges as an atom of hydrogen has on Earth. We do not know why this is. Why is the proton in the hydrogen atom 1,836 times as heavy as the electron? Davies points out that, "the actual values which the quantities assume turn out to be of crucial significance for the structure of the physical world."

So it would appear that the delicate balance of elements necessary to sustain life in the universe, elements which occur in exactly the right amount at every moment in time, without wavering, would supply the best evidence for a grand design. The possibility of that happening purely by accident is infinitesimal.

Is it possible that all this amazing synchronicity is accidental? I suppose that is a remote possibility. However, Davies (who is a mathematical physicist) in another book titled *Are We Alone?*, calculated that the odds against random permutations of molecules assembling DNA are about $10^{40,000}$. That would equate to tossing a coin and having it come up heads roughly 130,000 times in succession. Davies also quotes astronomer Fred Hoyle as saying that the high improbability of the formation of life by accidental molecular shuffling would be like "a whirlwind passing through an aircraft factory and blowing scattered components into a functioning Boeing 747." Possible? I guess it can't totally be ruled out, but it seems highly unlikely to me and to Davies and Hoyle. Both men are respected scientists.

So that is why I believe that the universe was created by design and not by accident, and that forms the basis for my own philosophy about God. Another interesting part of my philosophy relates to the interchangeability of particles. This also comes from Davies book *Are We Alone?*, in which he discusses the fact that the element carbon, which is the element on which all life is based, was not present in large amounts in the beginning, after the big bang. He proposes that the common elements such as carbon, oxygen, and iron came from the explosion of stars. He goes on to say that "the all important elements in our bodies, such as carbon, were once inside a star. Each carbon atom of your body was once sitting inside a star somewhere and got blown out, probably in one of those supernova explosions."

Now, that may not matter in the least to many people. For those who rely on faith alone for their belief in God, this may be just extraneous speculation. Even those of us who follow the scientific explanation must encounter faith at some point. There is a point beyond which facts remain hidden, and perhaps always will. However, the danger for me in simple faith alone is that we can use it to support just about any action we choose. We use it today to say that some people who live good lives are going to heaven and some who live good (or even better) lives are going to hell. We use it to blame God for things that we should be taking responsibility for ourselves (it is God's will that my child was killed by a drunk driver). My philosophy asserts that God gives us only beauty and love. Violence is a product of our own free will choice.

It seems odd to me that some people who claim to believe that God gave us free will choice also believe that everything that happens to us is because of God's will and not our own. Of course, God plays a role in my philosophy through the arrangement of particles. When particles combine to form a tornado, that is certainly outside the realm of my own will. In other words, God, not I, controls the action of nature, but I, not God, control my own actions.

You may wonder how this philosophy deals with the teachings of Jesus Christ. My belief system also encompasses the concept of simultaneous multidimensional realities. In other words, there are different levels of existence, all occurring at the same time. A belief in the *possibility* of this concept of multiple realities is also shared by such prominent scientists as Stephen Hawking, Richard Feynman and Murray Gell-Mann, according to a poll by political scientist L. David Raub. He polled seventy two leading cosmologists and other quantum field theorists, asking if they believed there are many worlds instead of just one, with the following results: 58% said yes it is true, 18% said no, it is not true, 13% said maybe it is true, and 11% had no opinion. For me, this belief opens up the explanation for the appearance of angels in this dimension: they can cross into our 3 dimensional world (and I believe they do) but we can't cross into theirs—yet.

I believe that God sent Jesus to correct our thinking about how we should live in order not to destroy ourselves; to help us get our exercise of free will choice back on track. By using Jesus as God's representative on earth, I am able to refer to God as "he". Otherwise God as I describe him is neither he nor she and would have to be referred to as "it," which is definitely awkward.

Many people have seen spirits from other dimensions—it is surprising how many people will admit to it if you open the door to that discussion. Most of them are reluctant to admit it before they know you think in those terms, lest you label them crazy. Anyway, while visions of angels (spirits) tend to come and go on a temporary basis, Jesus had a mission that required a longer stay on this plane and therefore a human body. What is so hard to understand about that? When he appeared to his disciples after the crucifixion, it is reported that they did not recognize him at first. I would submit that was because he came back briefly as a spirit (a regular angel). That isn't hard to understand either if you follow the particles/ waves line of reasoning. Is he coming again? If he does, people will probably not recognize him or pay any more attention to his words than they do now.

I believe the purpose of life is to create beauty in our lives. Following the teachings of Jesus helps us to do that. Jesus is not the only one to teach love and peace, of course, but his are the teachings that make the most sense to me. There are many ways to create beauty in our lives, but the most important way is by having beautiful relationships with our families, our friends, and others with whom we come in contact. That means we treat everyone with respect, and we help others in need whenever we can. We make our physical surroundings as clean and

attractive as possible, to the limit of our
resources. But primarily, we create beauty
through our relationships.

Jesus' teachings are simple but we humans
seem to find them impossible to follow, such
as the Ten Commandments: love your
neighbor and forgive his trespasses, don't
judge others—leave that to God. Many of
those who claim to be followers of Christ
steal, cheat, leave their families without
support, criticize everyone who doesn't
believe the same as they do, grasp their
riches to their bosoms and leave others to
starve The thing that bothers me most is
that many people behave as though the most
important thing in this life is to become as
rich as they can and leave the poor to wallow
in their own misery. Jesus never said that. In
fact, his words were: "The love of money is
the root of all evil."

The question this raises is, how does the soul
fit into all this? Since I believe that all
particles, including mine, are part of God, I
believe that the soul is that part of my
consciousness that speaks to God. That is, it
is my connection to the rest of the particles

in the universe; it is the part of my mind that attempts to control the ego, which often has a tendency to follow the ugly instead of the beautiful. The ego wants to do "whatever feels good," while the soul says, "wait, what you are contemplating will create ugliness and not beauty." The soul is the conscience, which always knows right from wrong and always tries to push us in the direction of right, in the direction that Jesus told us to follow.

The concept of the soul leads to another major part of my philosophy. I believe that each of us is born with a role to play in the care and maintenance of the world in which we live, in the care of our fellow earth travelers, in the care of the planet, and in the care of the universe as a whole.

I suppose this philosophy might be viewed as trying to capture the flavor of the Garden of Eden. In fact, the "Eden Philosophy" is a good name for it. With any philosophy it is important to ask, "if everyone followed this belief system, would it be a better world, a happier world?" If the answer is "yes", then it is a system worth pursuing. In the case of

the Eden Philosophy it is pretty clear that it
would create a happier, healthier world. The
Eden Philosophy, if believed and followed,
would lead us away from violence and toward
peace.

The question then becomes, how can we
persuade people to adopt this philosophy?
Maybe all we can do is try. Jesus faced the
same problem when he tried to change the
world. People have given lip service to his
teachings, but they have not put them into
practice in any large scale way. There is a
group of Christians out there with signs and
buttons reading WWJD (what would Jesus
do?) But society (including some Christians)
just scoffs at them or worse, ignores them.
Unfortunately, some of those wearing
buttons behave badly as well. That does not
mean the question is not a valid one which
can serve as a guide to better behavior for
everyone.

It is my conviction that many adults are too
ego-bound to listen to their souls. Our real
hope lies with the children. They are able
to suspend their disbelief while adults are
often hide-bound skeptics—we can teach the

children how to access their souls to guide their decisions. We can also show them how to live by Jesus' teachings. Will we? Not unless there is a major catastrophe that causes us to look for a source of comfort larger than ourselves.

The horror of 9/11 touched only 3,000 families directly, and now it has faded into our "wasn't it awful" file. So a real societal change, absent a huge catastrophe, will need to rely on parents teaching their children how Jesus meant us to live. That means parents will have to serve as role models, just as Aunty and Uncle served as my role models. It means that they must learn to discuss their differences in a respectful way. It means that when their child does something bad at school, parents must support the school authority and not threaten a lawsuit if the child is punished. It is absolutely shameful how today's parents refuse to believe their child could possibly have done anything wrong. It renders the school system impotent in maintaining any semblance of order for fear of a lawsuit. That needs to stop and each local PTA should take it on as a major project.

While we are on the subject of parents, it would be wonderful if they were to teach their children how to behave in public. How many times do we have to endure children running amok in restaurants, yelling and knocking things over, while parents sit and eat quietly as if nothing is happening? We tolerate children running up and down the aisles at a community performance, laughing, stomping their feet and disrupting the performers, while parents sit idly by. I find this totally unacceptable—a characteristic of our increasingly uncivilized society—there is no beauty being created here. The seeds of violence appear all around us.

We put up with road rage, where people are driving far past the speed limit, and/or talking on their cell phones, cutting in front of us so close that we have to slam on the brakes to avoid an accident. I have noticed in Los Angeles that hardly anyone stops at stop signs anymore. Breaking the law has become more and more acceptable which means that eventually we will become a completely lawless society. Extreme, you say? Anarchy begins with contempt for the law. This is a form of violence.

But this chapter is about the development of the Eden Philosophy and the creation of beauty. What did I learn during this period? I learned that God is real to me; that I can access that superpower through my own soul, and that I have a mission to pursue in this life, as I believe everyone does. We have but to ask and listen for the answer to know what that mission is; then we must have the courage to follow the directions we are given.

In the beginning, when I first discovered that I believed this, I was afraid to ask. I was afraid I would be given a task or mission that I would not want to do—that I would be asked to do something to change my life in a way I would not like. But now I know that will never happen. God never gives me anything that is not in my best interest, nothing that I cannot do, and nothing that I will be unhappy doing. We should never be afraid to ask.

CHAPTER 7

During the years I spent working all this out, I was becoming more receptive to the fascinating world of psychic phenomena. The group surrounding Nana (the psychic mentioned earlier in this book) as she was developing her psychic powers watched her prove, time after time, that she had a connection to the spirit world through a friendly "spirit guide." Many who watched were still skeptical until one day she told her boss something that his grandmother had said to him when he was a child— something not one other person knew. They began to use her to guide them in their investments, and they began to make money. Then one day her guide told her that she must not use her talent for making money, and that if she continued to do that she would lose her psychic gift. She stopped, of course, and began to use her powers to help people with their personal lives, without charge.

Nana's group of followers was small, and they
held séances on occasion, just to see if they
could make contact with the spirit world as
a group. They could, and they did. One
member of the group has a flower pressed
in a picture frame that came from a séance.
When I asked her about it she described the
incident. They were sitting in a circle,
holding hands and asking for a sign that the
spirits were present. Suddenly they felt
something soft dropping on their heads and
bodies. When they turned on the lights the
room was covered with flowers. No one had
left the room, and no one else was in the
house. It was an event that none of them
will ever forget. At another séance, when
they turned on the lights they found a
fishbowl with a live fish swimming in it. It
was not in the room when the séance began.

I regret that I was not at any of the more
exciting séances. However, I did attend one
that brought together my ideas about God.
The room was a conference room in an
office building in Century City. It was very
dark and we were waiting for something to
happen. Suddenly I saw a ball of light flitting
around the room near the ceiling. As I

watched it I began to wonder what it was. Then it dawned on me that it was clearly light and energy.

As I progressed from light and energy to particles and waves, I began to realize that the ball of light represented God. That was the seed from which the Eden Philosophy was born. God is light and energy, protons, photons and electrons. God is frequently defined as omnipotent (having unlimited power), omniscient (knowing everything), and omnipresent (present everywhere at the same time). Before the Eden Philosophy was born I could never figure out how God could be everywhere at the same time. This solved that problem for me.

There is a poem in a book written by Frank Tipler, titled, *The Physics of Immortality*, that best captures the flavor of an omnipresent God. It answers the question, "If a tree falls in the forest does it make a sound if no one is there to hear it?" The poem goes like this:

There once was a man who said,
    "God

Must think it exceedingly odd

If he finds that this tree

Continues to be

When there's no one about in the
   Quad.

Reply: Dear Sir: your astonishment's
   odd.

I am always about in the Quad.

And that's why the tree

Will continue to be,

Since observed by

Yours faithfully, God.

People sometimes ask me where this philosophy fits with the historical "isms" that the general public identifies with, that is, theism, pantheism, or deism. The answer is, it doesn't. It would conform to classical theism in its definition of God as omnipotent, omniscient, and omnipresent, and even the view of God as both transcendent (distinct from the universe) and immanent (residing within). But it departs from theism in that my description views God not as separate and apart from

the world, but as an integral part of the
world, with the soul as man's connecting link
to God.

Pantheism differs from theism in that it
sees God not as separate and distinct from
the world, but as purely immanent. My view
of God accepts the pantheistic view only in
part, because I see the world and man as
only a small part of a greater whole (the
universe).

Panentheism, a subset of Pantheism,is closer
to my view of God than the others; it sees
the world as a finite creation within the
infinite being of God. Panentheism also sees
God and man as co-creators of the future,
thus allowing for man's free-will choice, which
is a major component of my own philosophy.
In other words, God knows all of the past,
but knows the future as a set of possibilities
or probabilities.

Classical theism also claims a belief in man's
freedom to decide his own destiny, but that
view can be questioned whenever it is thought
that God knows the future, as theism
supposes. God's knowledge of the future

would seem to suggest predetermination, that is, that future events are predetermined by God, and man has no influence on them. This appears to me to be contradictory. If God knows the future, then the future is predetermined, which takes away man's free will choice.

For example, a man is sitting on a hill overlooking a river. The water passing directly in front of the man represents the present. The water downstream has already passed by him, so it represents the past. The water upstream has not yet reached him, so it represents the future. The man sitting on the hill is observing simultaneously the past, the present, and the future of the water passing by in the stream. The man can change the future path of the water by building a dam across the river, but whether or not he builds the dam is his decision. If God knows in advance that the man is going to build the dam, then the man no longer has free will choice to build it or not to build it.

The part of deism that fits with my own picture of God, is the idea that God established all the natural and moral laws necessary to keep the world operating properly. My picture differs from deism, however, where deism holds that man can understand these laws through his own reasoning powers and does not need any help from God to implement them. That would probably be true if man had no ego. But he does, so deism is not a compatible philosophy. My view of God as particles and waves seems to need an "ism" of its own.

I am not a physicist, and I do not claim to thoroughly understand the scientific concept of particles and waves. Norman Friedman, in *Bridging Science and Spirit,* explains that the world is made up of two elements—matter (particles) and fields (waves), and there are two types of fields—electromagnetic and gravitational—which act upon matter in certain ways. It appears that, at some point, matter takes on the characteristics of fields and fields take on the characteristics of matter. Some physicists believe that these changes depend upon the presence or absence of an observer. He goes on to say that when a single quantum particle is observed, it shows up as a particle, but when it is unobserved it seems to exist as a wave. I do not know enough about physics to expand on that. If you want to know more, you will need to read Friedman's book.

What this suggests to me, of course, is that nothing we see with the naked eye is quite as solid as it seems. Particles may be interchangeable across the universe. At least it seems logical to me that when we die our energy lives on in another plane. We know that energy, once created, cannot be destroyed, and since humans are bundles of energy that energy has to go somewhere. It suits me to believe that my energy finds a home on another level of existence. I'm not ready to speculate about what those levels might look like, but I suspect the level we now occupy is not near the top of the ladder!

The idea of multiple existing realities presents many intriguing possibilities for our after death experiences, as well as for certain experiences in this life. For example, suppose that when we are "born again," we are not simply reborn into our current earth reality but rather into another reality that presents us with a different set of learning experiences. And suppose that those multiple realities are hierarchical, with perfection leading us to higher and higher levels, eventually landing us in a state of nirvana.

It is a short imaginative step to view the highest level of reality as the home of angels. Angels, then, would have access to all levels of reality, and would be able to help those of us in trouble regardless of the reality in which we reside. They could be responsible for the "miracles" that many people around the world have witnessed. They could be responsible for the incredible "crop circles" that are still appearing all over the globe. These unexplained occurrences could be attempts on the part of angels to alert us to the existence of something higher than ourselves. That is the explanation that makes the most sense to me.

Why is it that we as a society (the few who do not simply scoff at them) are only willing to consider that they might have been made by people from other planets? People from other levels of reality would make a lot more sense to me. It also makes sense to think that inhabitants from other realities are trying to turn us from violence to beauty and love. Eventually, I think that the crop circles will bring us that kind of message.

For those of you who are fans of "Seth", the spirit channeled by Jane Roberts, here is what he says, in part, about simultaneous multidimensional realities: "God, therefore, is first of all a creator, not of one physical universe but of an infinite variety of probable existences, far more vast than those aspects of the physical universe with which your scientists are familiar."

The vast world of possibilities related to the spirit world, and what it might consist of fascinates and intrigues me. When I die, what will I find there? Will I wake up on a plane of existence that has none of my old friends and family? Will I remember this earth plane? Will it be a Garden of Eden, or will it be filled with problems and challenges like this plane clearly is? Will my particles coalesce as a recognizable person, or will they just float around like a gathering of gasses? We can only speculate. I find it interesting to contemplate.

What did I learn from my travels through the world of psychic exploration? I learned that there are truly people who can contact spirits outside this three-dimensional world, and that they are not all fakes. You can usually tell the difference by the amount of advertising they do, and the amount of money they charge for their services. As a society, we need to stop being afraid to discuss our otherworld experiences openly; it is surprising just how many people have had them.

All of this somewhat tortured discussion of angels and the spirit world, and of particles and waves, is simply an attempt to bring some level of understanding to those who have no vision of God, but who might be open to this particular vision. As I stated earlier in the book, those who are able to learn how to communicate with their soul, who can develop a belief in God in order to do that, will be much less likely to engage in violent behavior. You don't really need to understand all the "isms" of religious philosophy in order to find your soul, but some readers may find it interesting.

CHAPTER 8

Once I became immersed in the world of library administration, I never knew another 40-hour work-week. Management positions routinely require much more than 40 hours per week. I had little time for anything else; academic libraries are complex entities and I was responsible for about 400 staff and faculty, and the general operations of the libraries. During my tour of duty as second in command, librarians in the CSUC system were granted faculty status. That became a "sticky wicket," so to speak. Libraries are primarily administrative units, and while a few offer classes, most do not. However, librarians all have masters degrees and some have Ph.Ds. They are expected to do research, to write books and articles (though many do not), and to generally behave as academic faculty; academic faculty normally do not engage in administrative activities.

The trouble started, however, when university librarians really began to behave as academic faculty. Teaching faculty do not have administrative duties; librarians do. Teaching faculty do not have large numbers of staff to supervise; librarians do. Librarians must understand and provide for the research needs of all the students and faculty on campus; teaching faculty need attend to only their own classes. In short, librarians must respond to the policies established by the library administration (in consultation with library faculty, of course). It is up to the administration (in this case, me) to monitor and evaluate the adequacy of library services and to assure that the library budget is being spent in the most effective manner.

This is where the battles began. "Faculty," the librarians argued, "are not directed by administrators." They were correct, of course. "It will not do," the administration argued, "for each of the various departments in the libraries, all providing different kinds of services to the campus, to go off in whatever direction they choose, without regard to what all the other departments are doing; we will end up with chaos." And so it went throughout my remaining tenure at the University.

While I was still in the midst of the fracas, I decided to develop a labor cost analysis program to try and maintain the inadequate budget we had been reduced to by the State of California. Every year the State cut our personnel budget while the student body and the budget for books soared. My boss had given me orders (for the past several years) to figure out a way to live with the cuts with NO reduction in service. This took a great deal more than 40 hours a week. Worst of all, I ran smack into the "library faculty" issues. They had a fit when they learned that my labor cost analysis program required all staff, faculty, and administration (except my boss, of course) to make a daily accounting of their time spent on the job. "Faculty," they screamed, "do not account for their time!" They were right, of course, but I was the one charged with doing the impossible and it was my head that was on the block.

My boss ordered the project to go forward, and so it did. He had a saying that he lived by: "Behind every great man there is a woman in combat boots." He was the great man, I was the woman in combat boots. The project was finished, the results reported, and my staffing budget was tied to services. I could now say to the axe-wielding budget gurus, "Fine—your proposed cuts will require cuts in library service—you tell me which services you want to eliminate." It stopped the cuts. Eventually, the State adopted my labor cost analysis methodology statewide for the purpose of allocating library budgets. I had the two books mentioned earlier, detailing the program, published by JAI Press as part of their *Library and Information Science* series. This helped my career take off. I was beginning to be recruited for the position of Dean of Libraries at other universities.

But my scars were deep and my psyche was just plain tired. My boss expected me to do whatever was necessary to keep the organization running smoothly, to keep services to students and teaching faculty at a high level, while library faculty continued to assert their rights as academic faculty, unwilling to accept administrative direction and arguing about anything and everything. Finally, exhausted and frazzled, I gave up the battle and left the world of academia. Conversations with my soul told me that it was time to move on—to do something less stressful and more rewarding.

I had always wanted to take a trip around the United States, keep a journal of expenses, and then write a book about how to take a trip like that without spending much money. Since I didn't have much money, I would be the right person to undertake it. There was one serious handicap: I was a very minimal driver; I was fine if there was little traffic and there were no freeways. Fortunately, a friend who loved to drive was out of work at the time, had saved a little money, and said, "Let's go!" And go we did. With a small 4-cylinder truck and a mini-fifth wheel trailer we set off to see the country.

This was another great highlight of my life. There were no phones, no places we had to be, another friend back in Los Angeles was handling my meager bank account and paying my bills, and I was truly foot loose and fancy free. It was a most wonderful and memorable ten-month adventure. I was keeping track of every dime we spent, by category, and the final total at the end of the trip was $12 each, per day. That, I told myself, would make a perfect book. I had researched it carefully before we left and satisfied myself that no one had written anything like this, so I was sure it would be a best seller.

When we returned to California, broke but in wonderful spirits, I established my own small press and set out to write and publish *How to See the US on $12 per day (per person, double occupancy)*. The writing and publishing were the easy parts; what I did not know, but was soon to learn, was that the marketing of a small paperback by an unknown author was akin to pushing a baseball down the neck of a wine bottle.

After the book was printed and ready to distribute, I hired a publicist from Hollywood from whom I had taken a class on self-publishing before I left on the trip around the country. That, in itself, was a challenge. He took one look at the little paperback and wrinkled his brow. "I hate to disappoint you, but I don't think I can sell this book; I'm afraid I can't take you on as a client." I was crushed. How could he not see that this book was destined to be a best seller? Now, many years later, I understand that the book had the wrong title and the wrong cover but at the time I didn't get it. So I pleaded with him to take the book and at least try to get some radio/television coverage. Finally, reluctantly, he agreed.

A few weeks later I got a phone call from him; his voice was filled with incredulity as he sputtered, "I don't understand this—I really don't understand this—I am representing a book by a well known celebrity author and when I sent it out to the TV stations I threw in a copy of your book just to see if I got any comments on it. I can't believe this really happened, but "Hour Magazine" accepted your book for their show and rejected the other one!!"

Of course, I was ecstatic. Hour Magazine was a syndicated show with Gary Collins, and was very popular across the country. My co-author and I had a nice segment and the interview went off quite nicely. "Now," I said to myself, "this book is going to take off." Alas, it was not to be. The bookstores would not put it on their shelves because it was a single title, by a small press and unknown authors, and with an unattractive cover. I had several calls for books from around the country from people who had seen the show and had managed to find my press, but without bookstore exposure the book was doomed.

The interview itself was a wonderful experience, one that I will never forget. They were taping three episodes of Hour Magazine that day and all the interviewees were in a big room together, along with a huge table of food of every type imaginable. One of the people being interviewed was Vincent Price. I was a big fan of his, so this experience was well worth the cost of publishing the book! I had my own dressing room with my name on the door and a makeup person who made me gorgeous for the camera (well, maybe not gorgeous, but at least I felt important). It was a fun learning experience, but it didn't take long to realize that I was headed back into the job market.

I was broke, but I did not regret one single bit of it. I would urge everyone who hasn't planned such a trip to do so before your eyes grow dim and your knees give out!! I met a man in Florida who told me that he was 60 years old and about to look for a job. When I prodded him for more information, he told me that he had always believed that you should work until age 50, then stop and travel and do fun things, then go back to work at 60 and work until you drop. I like his thinking. The older I get, the more I enjoy productive work.

One important thing I learned was that it is not always best to stay with one profession all your life. Sometimes it just might be in your best interest to move on to new challenges and new adventures. The spirits become revived and your work becomes interesting and fun again. Most importantly, don't be afraid to try something new. Ask your soul for guidance, listen carefully for the answers, and then follow the directions you get.

CHAPTER 9

It was three years before I finally made a breakthrough in the search for work. I was overqualified for most management jobs, and I soon learned that (as one recruiter told me) librarians take a dim view of colleagues who have been out of their field for any length of time. Finally, a City Clerk, desperate for some management help, hired me as her assistant. The pay was pretty meager, so I kept looking. Within a year I had accepted a position as Manager of Information Systems for one of the city departments. This was also more than a 40-hour a week job, but I was just happy to have a job and a salary again.

This turned out to be another significant learning experience. It was my first time as manager of a union shop. The union was the United Auto Workers, and they smelled an easy mark: a librarian, a member of the faculty from the "soft underbelly" of academia, a writer. What could be more fun than twisting my tail? And twist they did. At least one grievance a week hit my desk, with three multi-million dollar lawsuits sprinkled in between. I survived them all. It didn't take long to figure out that if I carefully observed the requirements of the contract, I could write rules for performance and behavior, and enforce them. So I wrote rules, and I enforced them. Two lawsuits were eventually dismissed. The third one was rejected by the State Supreme Court, making the decision of the Court of Appeals (in my favor) the final word.

But in spite of all that, I enjoyed the challenges. My boss was a great guy and we did some pretty amazing things with the department. What had been a department nearly devoid of decent service to the public became a professional, well-respected, efficient unit. But once again it was time to move on. My boss was fired for political reasons, and I inherited a new boss who hated the sight of me. She berated me in front of my staff, publicly disapproved of my staff programs, embarrassed me at management meetings, and tried to eliminate my position from the budget. Fortunately, I enjoyed the confidence and strong support of the Agency's governing body so she was not able to do that. It was tough going, but I managed to stay until I was 62 and my pension was in place.

It was during those last few difficult years as Manager of Information Systems that I discovered a book titled *A Course in Miracles.* This book consists, along with a sizeable text, of 365 daily lessons for inner peace. It was not like any book I had ever read before, and it changed my life forever. Many of you have never heard of this book, because it is not advertised anywhere; it is spread by word of mouth (or from the writings of others). It is very difficult to explain, but I will try.

Some years ago a professor of psychology at Columbia University in New York began receiving uninvited thoughts from what appeared to be an outside source. They were thoughts quite foreign to her own background and knowledge so she tried to ignore them; but ultimately the message came, "Write this down; this is a course in miracles." The author eventually identified

himself as Jesus Christ. The professor had
been born a Jew, and this was all very
puzzling and difficult for her. However, at the
urging of her Department Chairman at
Columbia, she began to write down what was
being silently dictated to her. What emerged
was the 365-day series of exercises which
teaches many concepts, but in particular the
concept of God as the only true element in
our lives. The only real things in our lives
are the things that God gives us—everything
else is just a creation of our own minds, and
therefore unreal; nothing real can be
destroyed, nothing unreal exists.

This is a very simplified statement of what
lies in the text of this book. I completed the
entire set of 365 lessons, but not in one year.
Some lessons were particularly difficult for
me to grasp; for those, I had to spend several
days on one exercise. For example, I had
always believed that if I made up my mind
to do something, to achieve something,
nothing could keep me from doing it. I was
wrong. Now I understand that I do not have
control over everything in my universe.
Thinking that I did have control was foolish,
and it bumped into my belief in free will

choice. Put simply, if I have free will choice, so does everyone else. When my free will comes up against someone else's free will, neither of us has complete control. In other words, my right to punch Billy in the nose stops where Billy's nose begins. That is a critical concept in our relationships with other people. This exercise took about two weeks for me to grasp and to accept.

Gradually, I found myself experiencing inner peace while my personal world, the world immediately surrounding me, was in complete chaos as a result of the constant attacks on me by my boss. That was another major turning point in my life. The impulse to return insults with harsher insults, to lash out in defense of myself when attacked, began to fall into the "this whole scenario is meaningless" category. I was learning to put negative life experiences into proper perspective. When I retired from my position, I was awarded a Mayor's Commendation and, best of all, a plaque from my hard working, loyal staff.

Let me be clear, I do not believe in retirement. Leaving one's paid profession should not mean that it is time to stop being productive. The difference is that our efforts may, or may not, be rewarded with cash. Certainly anyone who wants to go into writing should not expect to get rich, though some do. Most do not. Clearly, my own life's mission is to write books about values: what can we do to make life more enjoyable for everyone? How can we give children the tools to make the right decisions? How can I convince society at large that it is imperative that we stop domestic violence, against children, against the elderly, against each other? I am compelled to pursue my mission, with or without cash rewards. We are surrounded by violence: violence in our popular music, in our movies, in our television shows, in the video games that kids play. Eventually, that constant drumbeat is translated into violent action against human beings.

The statistics are appalling. From an article in the *Los Angeles Times* of 7/10/95, titled "The Invisible Men", we read that 62% of teen mothers are prior victims of sexual abuse, primarily from stepfathers, mothers' boyfriends, family members, and others they trust; that 66% of children of teen mothers are fathered by adult men, 20 years old or older. Think about that. Is this acceptable behavior for a civilized society?

From a book by Dr. Jill Murray titled *But I Love Him,* we learn that 33% of teen girls are in an abusive dating relationship before they are out of high school; students from abusive homes are 25 times as likely to abuse their dates than those from non-abusive homes; 50% of dating women suffer physical, sexual, emotional, or verbal abuse from their dating partners; 35% of women who are killed in the U.S. are murdered by a boyfriend or husband, 25% of them are 15-24 years old; 90% of men in prison came from abusive homes. Stop and think about those awful statistics.

Why do we, as a society, allow this kind of barbaric behavior? It has to bear some relationship to our adherence to that old saying, "a man's home is his castle." Through the years we have believed that whatever happened behind closed doors was no one's business—that society has no business meddling in the private affairs of a family. It

is time for women to wake up and realize
that they need not and should not, accept
such behavior. There are women's shelters
to help abused women and children, and
there are local and county agencies where
they can get help. Most importantly, parents
should be teaching their children, by their
own behavior, that abusive behavior is not
acceptable.

After I left the field of management, I
moved to my home in the mountains and
began to write full time to address the
problems that still haunted me: the issue of
what to do for abused children who have no
help because they have no visible scars or
bruises, and how to explain in a way that
children can understand and accept, the idea
that God is a very real entity with whom they
can communicate. I knew that I was destined
to write books in order to pursue the mission
I had been given, but how could I put these
very complicated issues into books that
children would be willing to read?

After much soul searching, I concluded that
I would use animals to convey my messages,
and that I would write in a fable format. But

which animal? How could the ideas be presented? How could an animal know what human children needed to know? I pondered. I stared out the window a lot. Finally, my soul produced the answers.

The one animal that can, and does, live in the midst of human habitation, is the opossum. 'Possums, as we called them in the Ozarks, can hang by their tails (although admittedly upside down) and can presumably peer into windows of houses if they choose. They often live in the midst of big cities and somehow manage to survive.

I got the idea when I was living at the beach, in a city of one square mile with a population of 19,000. To say it was a wall-to-wall city is an understatement. Yet, late one night as I was coming into my garage, down the steps on the other side of the street came a very large, very fat, 'possum, headed straight for my open garage door. I quickly closed the door just seconds before the 'possum took up residence in my garage, and at that moment I knew which animal would be the focal point of my fables.

And so, P.J. Pokeberry, 'possum author, was born. The first book, *The Secret of Hilhouse*, talks to kids about what God looks like, why it is important to listen to your soul and not your ego, why you shouldn't do something just because everyone else does it, why you should listen to your parents even though they don't always make the best decisions themselves, and other hard issues. Then, the other main character, a metaphysical frog named "Ribbit" is introduced. The book is meant to be read by parents and children together, so that important life issues can be discussed—hopefully, so that parents can explain their values and can also learn the values their children hold; they are not always the same.

Once again I had to face the critical question, "who is going to publish this small paperback that contains no violence, was written by an unknown author, and talks about God?" The answer was pretty clear: I would have to publish this one myself—again. I got a friend to illustrate it and another friend who was a licensed Marriage and Family Counselor to write the introduction, and set about once again to publish something that I believed was important to say, whether anyone bought it or not. As before, I had good publicity—a number of radio and television interviews and some excellent reviews, but bookstores would not put it on their shelves. Some readers managed to find it anyway and I had very positive feedback, particularly from grandparents who were having great difficulty communicating with their grandchildren about values.

The second book by P.J. Pokeberry, titled *The Huckenpuck Papers*, is a book about domestic violence and includes the recommended program to help abused kids I mentioned earlier in this book. Once again, Ribbit, the metaphysical frog with connections to the universe (read God) gives the children sage advice about important issues. The abortion issue is discussed openly, and the decision-making process in this critical stage of a young person's life begins with "ask your soul for direction."

Of course, the natural question that will follow this advice is, "how will I know if the answers I get are really from my soul, or just my head telling me what I want to hear?" The answer to that is simple: if the consequences of following that answer might hurt yourself or someone else, the answer did not come from your soul; God only gives us answers that are good for ourselves and others.

It did not take long to realize that I was never going to find a publisher for anything this far out of the mainstream, especially since kids would never just walk into a bookstore and pick up a fable about a 'possum and a frog. They want excitement and adventure, mystery and violence. So once again my book was self-published. A series of radio interviews yielded few sales and I finally realized that the interviews were on programs catering to business people—definitely the wrong audience. So I gave up the publicity route and began talking to people personally about the need for a program for emotionally and psychologically abused children. Book publishing is only useful to me if it advances the mission I have been given.

In the meantime, on a trip to Palm Springs with a friend, I stayed in a popular spa that provided programs on a variety of topics for guests. While I don't usually bother with psychics who give readings for money, I thought this was probably the most interesting program of the lot. Early in the program I began to suspect that this particular psychic might have some credibility, so I scheduled a private session for later that afternoon. I never told her anything about myself.

When I sat down with her, there was a long silence and then she said, "In all my years of doing this I have never seen so many spirit guides around anyone. You are surrounded by them. One of them is your grandmother; they are all here to protect you while you pursue the mission you have been given." That got my attention. I had never mentioned my grandmother, or a mission, or anything else.

She went on, "I don't know what your mission is, but it must be a very important one. Whatever it is, it was planned a long time ago on another plane of existence." I remained silent and she continued. "Your mother, your father, and your grandmother planned for the time, place, and circumstances of your birth.

Your father was a hard sell because he did not want to have a family life; he wanted to be footloose and fancy free to live life as he chose. They agreed that he would only have to provide the necessary sperm, without benefit of marriage and family entanglements, and your mother would do the rest. (The psychic did not say how rape was chosen as the means to accomplish this.) Your grandmother was also to play a role, probably a protective role."

By this time, I was speechless. I didn't have to be careful not to tell her anything she could use because she didn't need me to tell her anything. She went on to say that my mother was not one of my spirit guides because she had had a very hard life and had gone far away to rest for a very long time. I didn't need her to tell me that my mother had a hard life; I knew that first hand. But the rest was not something I would ever have thought about. At one point I asked her to tell me something about my father and she said he was dark, with dark hair, and very handsome. She also said that he was a hobo, he loved to ride the rails, and that he had died in an accident on a train.

That trip to Palm Springs was one I will never forget. There is never any proof that messages like this are true. It is difficult to believe that this person, knowing nothing about me or my past, could have spun such a tale and have it be consistent with everything I know about my family. It has caused me to focus more intently on my mission and its progress. At times it seems like I am on the wrong track because my efforts seem to have no positive results. Then I ask for guidance in my meditations and the message is always, "stay the course."

What did I learn in this phase of my life? I learned so many lessons that I would not know where to begin. Probably the most important one is that when God gives you a mission, don't ask too many questions. Follow the path that opens to you; don't worry about failures; don't be discouraged; just keep putting one foot in front of the other. Eventually, the rock will be moved forward and it will get you closer to your mission. And yes, you have a mission, too. Do you know what it is? Have you asked?

CHAPTER 10

Part of the impetus for writing about domestic violence is not just my own psychological trauma resulting from six years of terror as a child, it is also about the question of why women put up with abuse. Why do they stay in a relationship year after year and suffer in silence? I found a partial answer in my mother's diary.

I knew that my mother had kept a diary because over the years when she was showing me a new dress or suit in her closet, or a quilt she was working on, she would take the diary off the shelf and say something like, "This is my diary." I never asked to read it and she never offered. After she died and I was packing up her things, I ran across the diary. It was locked. I debated with myself whether I should now force the book open and read it. Certainly I was curious, especially about the details of my early childhood of which I had only selected memories. But it was locked, after all, and I could not bring myself to break into it. I put it away in my cedar chest with some of her other belongings.

A year later I was looking in the chest for something and picked up the diary to move it out of the way. As I picked it up, the key fell out. "Thanks Mom," I said, and opened it. As I read it I noticed that it only covered the four years prior to her marriage to Pop. I expected to find out what her life was like as a housekeeper, what she thought of me, what other jobs she had during that period (I knew she had been a hotel maid for awhile), things about her life in general. I learned nothing of those things. I was mentioned twice in the book, once when Aunty took me shopping and again when she said (before I came to live with her), "I miss my kid." The rest of the book was about Pop.

It was clear that she had thought of nothing else during those four years. "We had a date tonight but he showed up drunk and I wouldn't go." Or, "He didn't show up for our date—he is probably drunk somewhere." At one point his drinking became such a problem that she threatened not to see him again. But he came to apologize and make some lame excuse for his bad behavior and she recanted. The handwriting was clearly on the wall, but her devotion to him was so deep that she couldn't see the danger that lay ahead for her. In retrospect, I believe she would have married him anyway, even if she had known.

So one of the things that keeps a woman in an abusive relationship is a kind of blind devotion to a man whom she is certain is going to change his ways and become what she wants him to be. As a friend of mine is fond of saying, "people continue to do the same thing, while expecting the outcome to be different." It doesn't work that way. If you want to change the final result, you have to change your behavior. In this case, she should have changed her behavior and walked away because it was certain that he was not going to change his.

I think the other reason she stayed with him was because she was sure in her own mind that no other man would want to marry a woman with a small child born under dubious circumstances. Her self-esteem was nearly non-existent. This appears to be true of most women and girls in abusive relationships. Abuse itself breeds self-contempt. Nathaniel Branden, a well known writer on the issue of self-esteem, said he couldn't think of a single psychological difficulty that is not traceable to poor self-esteem, including anxiety, depression, fear of intimacy or success, alcohol or drug abuse, underachievement at school and work, spousal abuse, child molestation, emotional immaturity, suicide, and crimes of violence.

Still, the anti-intellectual snobs continue to deride the notion that we need to work at developing self-esteem in our young people. To any thinking person it is clearly a matter that begs for a major effort to try and correct this problem in our youth population. *It was important enough to me to sit down and think through what kinds of actions might help kids and to write "The Ten Commandments of Self Esteem" for them. Here they are:*

1. **Recognize that you are unique.** You can't be exactly like anyone else, and no one else can be exactly like you. Honor that uniqueness. Most of us go

through life trying to be just like everyone else. When we can't be, we think there is something wrong with us instead of remembering that we are not supposed to be just like **anyone** else. Each of us is unique.

2. **Accept the fact that you aren't perfect,** and neither is anyone else. But focus on those parts of you that are your strengths, and develop them to the fullest extent possible. Work on your less than perfect areas too, but don't dwell on them. View them as just something to work on.

3. **Establish your values early in your life, and live by them.** Begin with a deep respect for life, and for everything that God created—for the animals, for the world around you, and especially for people. Respect God's creations as you would respect God.

4. **Keep the Bible's Ten Commandments by your bedside and read them each night before you go to sleep.** These are universal values that will serve you well

throughout your lifetime. "Don't kill anyone, don't steal, don't lie, love your neighbors and don't judge them, and honor your parents." These are basic values that are required for self-esteem.

5. **Never do something just because everyone else is doing it.** Self-esteem is simply knowing that you have done your very best to keep your actions consistent with your values—to walk away from pressures applied by others to get you to abandon your own values and accept theirs. People want others to accept their values because it validates them. Don't pursue values that are contrary to your own.

6. **Respect yourself.** It is tempting to believe that you get respect from others by doing what they want you to do. They might pretend to *like* you if you do what they want you to do, but they won't *respect* you. And they won't like you for very long either, because we can't really like someone we don't respect. So, if you want respect from others, you must respect yourself.

7. **Use your talents.** Every person comes into the world with a talent for something. We are not all destined to compose great symphonies, or to write a bestseller, or to invent the world's greatest bread slicer. But if we listen to our inner voices, we will be guided to excel at something. And if we pursue that direction vigorously, our self-esteem will soar.

8. **Create beauty in your life in every way possible.** If you are familiar with the Bible's Old Testament, you will remember that God created a beautiful Garden of Eden for humans. Somehow, we lost track of the importance of beauty in our lives. We need to try and recreate the beauty represented by the Garden of Eden—in our music, our literature, our relationships, our environment, in every aspect of our lives. These are the kinds of things that make us feel good about our lives, and therefore about ourselves.

9. **Develop your mind.** Learn about other people of the world who live with

different customs and beliefs, and treat
those who are different from you with
respect. Make lifelong learning an
integral part of your life, for the more
you know the less likely you are to
abandon your humility. People with a
healthy self-esteem are humble. People
with low self-esteem are often arrogant
and disrespectful of others.

10. See yourself as part of a greater whole.
You live in a vast universe, filled with
beautiful and wonderful things. And
you are part of the beauty and the
wonder of it all. You are significant
because you are part of something
awesome and grand.

So remember that you are unique. Build
on your strengths, establish your values
early on and live by them; use the Ten
Commandments as a base; never do
something just because everyone else is
doing it; respect yourself and use your
talents; create beauty in your life; develop
your mind, and see yourself as part of a
greater whole. This is a positive recipe for
the development of self-esteem.

While these Ten Commandments were
written for young people, there are a lot of
adults who could use a good dose of self-
esteem, and these Ten Commandments will
work for anyone of any age. I think my
mother followed all of these rules except for
number 6 "respect yourself." That one might
have kept her from an abusive relationship,
but maybe it wouldn't have been enough.
Her devotion to Pop was so overwhelming
that even a good dose of self-respect might
not have saved her. After he died, she
became very ill. The doctor told her there
was nothing physically wrong with her, that
she was dying of a broken heart. He advised
her to come to California to visit me for
awhile. She took his advice and eventually
she overcame her grief at losing him. We
became acquainted for the first time, and
found that we really liked each other. After
he was gone, my mother and I became very
close friends. When she died, I was the one
with a broken heart.

CHAPTER 11

This book is primarily intended as a "call to arms" for all subversives, as well as for all those who want to "overthrow" our current permissive social attitudes toward, and acceptance of, violence. It doesn't seem likely that we could force the government to develop a program to reduce violence, but we could, indeed in my mind we must, take it upon ourselves to change our violent, corrupt society. The government can't do that for us by passing laws; we must do it ourselves by changing what we permit and tolerate in the way of public, and in some cases private, behavior. By change, I mean we must find a way to stop the violence against women, children, and the elderly. We must stop accepting music in our homes and lives that is violent and demeaning to women. We must stop accepting violence in our movies, television programs, and video games. We must stop teaching children that girls are second-class citizens. We must stop telling women that they must be subject to their husbands, and women must stop believing that. All these things sow the seeds of violence.

This is a tall order, but it can be done. Women have far more power than they choose to exercise, more than they believe they have. Let's look at these issues one by one. First, stop the violence against women, children, and the elderly. This has to begin with women teaching their children that violence is not acceptable, and by exhibiting proper behavior by demanding a respectful relationship among all the members of the home. If dad/mom exhibits disrespectful and/or abusive behavior and refuses to participate in the "peaceful household" idea, start looking for a job (if you don't have one) and move out, taking the kids with you. This requires a paradigm shift, from "I can't be happy without all the luxuries that two incomes provide," to "the most important thing in life is to live in a respectful atmosphere where the dignity of each member of the family is honored."

It is estimated that approximately 3.3 million kids in the U.S. between 3 and 17 years of age are at risk of exposure to family violence. This is appalling and totally unacceptable. Women can stop it by refusing to stay in an abusive environment. If enough women refuse, men will eventually change. It must be noted that some women are violent as well. Men who are abused must follow the same path, that is, refuse to stay in an abusive environment.

Sometimes people stay in abusive relationships because they become accustomed to the comforts provided by two incomes. If they leave the relationship, they will probably have to lower their standard of living—or work two (or three) jobs. The availability of money—the accumulation of wealth—becomes more important than the abuse suffered by one of the partners and, sadly, more important than the welfare of the children who are damaged by living in that kind of environment.

Remember this admonition? "It is easier for a camel to go through the eye of a needle than for a rich man to enter the kingdom of heaven." Why would Jesus make such a pronouncement? Not because money is evil.

Good and evil refer to actions, and since money is inanimate, it can't be good or evil. But what happens to humans is that we become addicted to money at the expense of everything else—our families, our friends, our own wellbeing. The more we have, the more we find that it isn't enough. The more toys we have, the more toys we need: a bigger car, a television in every room, a bigger house; that cycle needs to be broken.

We can begin to create change by vowing to buy only replacements for worn out equipment and appliances; we can use the money we save to help a friend who is having financial difficulties—or, we can use it to allow one partner to leave an abusive relationship. Perhaps it would even be possible to save enough to allow one parent to stay at home and teach values to the children. Maybe that parent could volunteer some time in public agencies that need help. There is plenty of work to do.

The other thing that a woman can and should do before she marries, is to make sure she has the skills to make enough money to support herself and her children in case the marriage turns abusive. Young women can begin to do that now, today. Sure, you're madly in love. So was my mother. But it is important to remember this frightening statistic that I mentioned earlier: 35% of women who are killed in the U.S. are murdered by a boyfriend or husband, 25% of them are 15-24 years old. Women must also be aware that those who leave their abusive partners are 75% more likely to be killed by their abusers than those who stay in the relationship, and leaving must be carefully arranged and coordinated with law enforcement so that the danger is reduced as much as possible.

It is far easier to refrain from dating or marrying a man (or woman) who exhibits any signs of possessiveness and jealousy and/ or who has an alcohol or drug problem. This is called early prevention. Women in this country can change this world of violence by standing together and refusing to permit it. Will we? That remains to be seen.

In the case of abuse of the elderly, some of this happens in the home of an offspring and some in nursing homes. You stop it in the home by simply not accepting it. If anyone in your home is abusing an elderly person, insist that the behavior be stopped and if that doesn't work, talk to someone in your local family services agency to see how they can help.

The best way to stop it in nursing homes is to visit the relative there often and observe their living conditions. Talk to others in the home and get a feel for what goes on there. If you know an elderly person who has no family to look in on them, you might visit them occasionally, too. We seem to have lost the idea that we were once a kind and caring nation, and that kind and caring is a desirable state of affairs. You and I can do something about that.

The next thing we can do is to stop the violent music that is demeaning to women and degrading to all who hear the ugly language used. Oh sure, the party line is, "well, it is what all the kids listen to so I can't deny mine the opportunity to listen too." Oh yes, you can. As a parent you can refuse to allow your children to buy it, and you can refuse to allow them to play it in the home.

If you catch them with one of those CDs, cut off their allowance for a period of time, or find some other way to let them know that you mean business. Of course you can't stop them from hearing it when they are visiting their friends who play it, but if women across the country would support this effort, there wouldn't be any friends who were playing it. If parents and kids stop buying it, the recording companies will stop making it. That is the only way this kind of problem can be addressed. Let me repeat: IF PEOPLE STOP BUYING THESE CDs, THE RECORDING COMPANIES WILL STOP MAKING THEM.

We must also stop the violence in our movies, television programs, and video games. The party line on this one is, "I can't do anything to stop these movies and games from being produced—what do you want from me?!" My response once again is, yes you can. Parents can stop their children from going to violent movies—know what the movies are about and draw the line. Will they slip away and see one sometimes anyway? Of course they will. But when they do, they will know that you do not approve, and you will have told them the reason why you do not approve so they will at least understand that the movies are unhealthy and they should not be there.

In the case of television violence, it will take a major change in lifestyle to fix this problem. First, children watch far too much television. Parents can direct them toward more positive activities, such as reading books, and that must be done in order to address this problem. My cousin has a child who is very bright, very talented, and loves to read. He plays basketball, soccer, piano, and the cello. He has only been allowed to watch one television program per week, which his parents choose. He is the most well adjusted child I have ever known. Partly, I'm sure, because the parents don't watch much television either. The family does things together: they hike, go camping, clean up the yard together, play games together in the evening, read together. Imagine this, not one member of that family has died because they don't watch endless television. This change can be made, but parents will have to make it happen.

It is important to understand that the only thing people in other countries know about

Americans is what they see in the movies and television programs we produce. Is that really what we want our image to be around the world? I certainly don't. Is it any wonder that people in the Arab world hate us? Of course they view us as totally corrupt; we are all Tony Soprano in their minds. We must stop ignoring that reality and do something about it. Can we? Of course we can. Will we? It is up to all of us to fix it.

And then there are video games. This is dealt with the same way you deal with violent, ugly CDs. You do not allow your children to buy them or download them. Children should not be allowed to go to video arcades either. About now, some of you are saying, "wait a minute—this is just something kids do—my kids are not going to be denied access to what every other kid gets to do." Or, "kids have rights too—they have a right to choose to do what everyone else is doing." No, they don't. Kids have a right to a safe, healthy home environment; they have a right to adequate food and clothing; they have a right to a good education; they have a right to loving parents. They do not have a right to do anything they please. If that is the way they behave (doing whatever they please) it is because the parents have given them the right and not because it comes with the birth certificate.

Far too many parents have abdicated their responsibility for decision-making and dumped that responsibility on their children. If we are to achieve a reasonable level of civility in this society, parents must begin to accept responsibility for the behavior of their children. We begin at home by establishing and exhibiting proper values and behavior, and we augment that by not allowing bad public behavior to pass without showing some disapproval of it. Sometimes a disapproving frown will suffice, sometimes a quiet word to parents whose children are racing and yelling through the restaurant. They won't thank you for it, but perhaps it will make them think about it.

Our training of young girls is also woefully lacking. We allow boys in the families to have special privileges far more than the girls. We encourage boys to excel at sports, but not the girls. We expect the boys to grow up and become corporate executives, but not the girls. If girls want to play sandlot baseball, we should support and encourage that. If boys want to take cooking classes, we should support and encourage that.

Only by treating boys and girls equally in all areas will we be able to develop strong self-esteem in our girls. Right now that is not happening. As a result, 33% of girls are in an abusive dating relationship before they are out of high school. Why do they tolerate that? Because they are not taught at home that violence is not okay, and that they should never accept that kind of treatment. Beyond high school, 50% of dating women suffer physical, sexual, emotional or verbal abuse from their dating partners. Why is that? Because abused teens grow up to allow themselves to be abused adults. Some religions actually teach that the Bible expects women to be "subject to their husbands." That exacerbates the problem. Married people should be equal partners in their marriage.

We continue to wring our collective hands and rail against the movie industry, the music industry, the television industry, because they

are corrupting our children. The truth is we
could stop it if we had the will to do it. These
industries are simply pandering to the moral
and intellectual deficiencies of our parents
who pass those moral and intellectual
deficiencies on to their children by allowing
them to consume the corporate garbage.
Family values, good or bad, are passed on
to the next generation which passes them
on to the next, and the next, and so on.
Whether our values trend toward more and
more violence, more and more degradation,
is up to us. They could just as easily trend
toward less and less violence, less and less
degradation. It will take a major, widespread
movement to change direction, but it is
possible.

CHAPTER 12

The discussion of violence cannot be finished without an evaluation of the effects of music on behavior. Studies clearly show that classical music helps children learn math and science more easily. It improves their SAT scores and it causes children to be less disruptive in a school setting. We have largely eliminated orchestral music from the schools in this country, and that is a serious mistake. In California, only 10% of public schools offer orchestral music classes. This appears to be a national trend. As a result, symphony orchestras around the country, and in California, are going out of business due to lack of support. Orchestras that have been in business for more than a century are having to close their doors. The San Jose Symphony and the Glendale Symphony are two of several tragic closures, and others are in danger of going under.

Some people say it is because the ticket prices are too high, but I do not think that is the real story. Millions of people pay far higher prices for tickets to sports events and rock concerts, so clearly it is not that people can't afford to attend symphony concerts. The real problem is that without this type of music in the schools, children do not grow up with a love of it and parents are not exposed to it because children no longer play these instruments. The problem is a lack of exposure, and this sad reality is going to lead us to the total loss of one of our most important cultural treasures. For centuries, classical music has been an essential ingredient of a civilized society. So was fine literature. Both of these things are going the way of the dinosaur and that is a tragedy.

Budget gurus in the public schools tend to look at orchestral music as an expensive leisure activity, rather than as an essential part of the curriculum. There are a number of scientific studies that how the importance of classical music to a child's learning processes.

1. Students with coursework/experience in music performance and music appreciation scored 104 points higher on the Scholastic Aptitude Test (SAT) than students with no arts participation.

2. Music training is far superior to computer instruction in dramatically enhancing children's abstract reasoning skills, the skills necessary for learning math and science.

3. In the Kindergarten classes, children who were given music instruction scored 48 percent higher on spatial-temporal skill tests than those who did not receive music training.

4. Students who can be classified as "disruptive" total 12 percent of the total school population. In contrast, only 8 percent of students involved in music classes meet the same criteria as "disruptive."

Here are a couple of examples of my own personal knowledge of instances where classical music played a role in reducing disruptive behavior:

In Coeur d'Alene, Idaho, the downtown merchants and restaurant owners were having a major problem with teen and young adult hoodlums creating havoc and driving away customers (playing loud rap music in their cars on the streets, drinking and throwing beer cans and bottles in the streets, etc.). The merchants were unable to find any way to get rid of the troublemakers, when one man suggested they put loud speakers outside all the shops and play loud classical music to drown out the rap music and vocal mayhem. Much to their surprise, it did not just drown out the other noises, the hoodlums left the area for good—they couldn't stand the calming effect of the music; they get their kicks from music that agitates, that excites and induces frenetic behavior. Bach was just too soothing for them.

The other situation I encountered was in a high school in central California. It was a school with 3,000 students, larger than some small cities. I was there at noon to confer with the school administration and I was literally shocked at what I saw. The campus was totally calm, neat, well-dressed students were milling about, going to lunch and coming back, there was no graffiti on walls or fences. There was no loud rap music coming from the cars in the parking lot; there was no gang attire; it was wonderful. I stopped to ask directions; the student was pleasant and helpful. I noticed that there was classical music playing from the outdoor loud speakers. I mentioned it to the principal and he said, "We always play classical music during lunch break and between classes—when the music stops, the kids know they have one minute to get to their class." What a simple way to have a quiet campus.

On the flip side, there is no such music taught or listened to in our local public schools. One day I called the junior high school and spoke with an administrator about our local orchestra sending a group of players over to play some classical pieces to demonstrate the different instruments. We had done that in the elementary schools and the kids loved it. Most of them had never even seen some of the instruments, much less have heard them played. The administrator said to me, "Oh no, we couldn't possibly allow that—the kids don't like classical music and they would be so disruptive that your people wouldn't be able to play." Needless to say, our musicians didn't play there.

There are some additional studies that I need to share with you that will explain further why the schools need to rethink their elimination of orchestral music:

1. An intensive series of studies carried out by a researcher in Denver, Colorado, demonstrated the effects of different kinds of music on a variety of household plants. The experiments were controlled under strict scientific conditions, and the plants were kept within large closed cabinets on wheels in which light, temperature, and air were automatically regulated. Three hours a day of acid rock, played through a loudspeaker at the side of the cabinet, was found to stunt and damage the plants in less than four weeks.

2. In another series of studies, the music of two different Denver radio stations was played to two groups of petunias. There was one rock station and one semi-classical station. Here is what the Denver Post reported about those studies:

> The petunias listening to the rock station refused to bloom. Those on the semi-classical station developed six beautiful blooms. By the end of the second week, the rock station petunias were leaning away from the radio and showing very erratic growth. The petunias having the semi-classical music were all leaning toward the sound—they grew and thrived. Within a month, all plants exposed to rock music died.

Let me repeat that in case you missed it: WITHIN A MONTH, ALL PLANTS EXPOSED TO ROCK MUSIC DIED. How sad that our young people are listening only to music that kills flowers.

In other studies, the head of the Botany Department at Annamalia University in India discovered not only that constant exposure to classical music caused plants to grow at twice their normal speed, but also went on to find what seemed to be one of the main causes of this accelerated growth. The sound waves caused increased motion in cellular protoplasm. What does this have to do with humans? Protoplasm is the basic material of which all plant, animal, AND human life is made up.

Most important from these studies is the finding that the LATER GENERATIONS of the seeds of musically stimulated plants carried the improved traits of greater size, more leaves, and other positive characteristics. MUSIC HAD ACTUALLY CHANGED THE PLANTS CHROMOSOMES! The significance of these findings to human society is profound.

As one researcher put it, "When used correctly, music is perhaps unequaled in its power to instill in man the beauty of true morality and those higher, inspired purposes for which our lives are intended." Confucius said this: "If one should desire to know whether a kingdom is well governed, if its morals are good or bad, the quality of its music will furnish the answer." That is certainly true today. The music we are listening to today speaks volumes about the state of our morals. This music clearly sows the seeds of violence.

Music may play a far more important role in determining the character and direction of a civilization than most people have until now been willing to believe. Throughout history, and in all parts of the world, music has been looked upon as a powerful force for good in the development of civilizations. Ours is a broken civilization, but it can be repaired. The path is obvious.

In one experiment conducted by psychologists, rats were given the free run of two separate but connected boxes. Music was piped into each of them—Bach into one and rock into the other. Though the two boxes were identical and all other conditions except the music were equal, the rats all spent their time in the Bach box. To test further the purity of the experimental conditions (to be sure that one of the boxes had not had cheese in it, or something like that), the music broadcast into the two boxes was switched; and gradually all the rats moved into the other box, which was now the Bach box. You see, even the rats know the difference.

If you want to read about these studies for yourself, see David Tame's book titled *The Secret Power of Music*. Every parent should be familiar with the important ramifications of these studies. You can begin in a very simple way to apply the benefits of classical music; you can buy some Mozart and Bach CDs and play them in your home—you don't have to wait for an enlightened school administration to put this music back in the school curriculum. That transformation will take time and a lot of parents demanding it. Yes, we can change the face of our society.

In my home town, several of us "retired" people are working hard to fill the gap left by the lack of orchestral music in the public schools. Our volunteer Community Orchestra plays all its concerts free to the public so that parents, regardless of income, can bring their children and expose them to this kind of music. Once exposed, children love the music, and many of them begin to want to study violin, or cello, or viola, or bass. The Orchestra's Concertmaster now teaches some 80 string students, conducts a junior string orchestra, and a private elementary school orchestra. She has several students who auditioned for the Community Orchestra, were accepted, and now are regulars in the Orchestra. In addition, one of her advanced violin students recently won a music scholarship to a prestigious university. All this has taken place quietly with no assistance or participation by the local School Board. Those of us who serve on the Orchestra's Board of Directors are deeply dedicated to these programs, which are supported entirely by donations, fundraisers, small grants, and the many hours of time the Concertmaster donates (at no charge) to the community's children. This is true commitment.

On a broader scale, we need to begin to work hard to preserve those elements of our cultural heritage that do not produce seeds of violence but which encourage the best in us. Those elements include classical music, both instrumental and choral, visual arts that uplift us rather than degrade us, old time fiddling that brings a joyous and positive flavor of our past, and crafts such as quilt making that remind us of our self sufficient past and which showcase our talents. We are in danger of losing those vital parts of our cultural heritage and replacing them with activities that create violence rather than beauty.

Please note that as immigrants pour into this country, they work hard to preserve the positive elements of their own cultures. Those of us with roots in Western Europe are sitting idly by while the beauty of our cultural heritage fades into history. What a shame it is that we are too busy in our pursuit of wealth and fame to care.

So those are the challenges to all of us. We can change our society in a positive way without a lot of effort, just a change of mind and a change of heart. We don't need laws to bring this about; we just need the cooperation and the determination of our citizens. Patriotism requires much more than attaching an American flag to everything with a flat surface. It requires a true dedication to doing whatever is necessary to lift up our collective morals and values. It means that we have to get off our duffs, turn off the television and make the changes that I have outlined above. It means spending time with our children, teaching them by both words and actions the important values we all SHOULD hold dear. It means caring about everyone in our society, and not just about ourselves. It means putting forth some effort to make the necessary changes.

Some of those necessary changes can be accomplished by changing our regressive mindset about retirement. We think that when we retire we should spend all our time pursuing our favorite hobbies—isn't that, after all, what retirement is all about—doing all those fun things we couldn't do while we were working?

My view of life is somewhat different. I believe that we need to give ourselves vacations, just as we did while we were gainfully employed, although perhaps a bit more. The rest of the time should be spent making our community better, more productive in its service to its citizens, more beautiful, more peaceful. We are living much longer lives now, progressively more as time passes. Can you really spend the next 20 or 30 years doing nothing but playing bridge and golf? How about traveling for 10 years and spending the next 10 or 20 years doing something satisfying and useful? I'm not saying, "don't have any fun," I am saying, "have fun, but do some useful things too." My experience has been that getting volunteers for community projects is limited to a few dedicated souls who carry an enormous burden on behalf of the entire community. It should not be this way. We will never change our society for the better that way. Imagine what would happen if each person did just one thing to improve the community!

So arise subversives and non-subversives!! Make your presence felt through changes in your own home, through your local elected governing boards, your PTA, and other service clubs. Volunteer some time for helping your local police, your family service centers, your local hospital, or your battered women's shelter. There is a ton of work to do. Wave the flag of volunteerism along with your American flag. That is the true essence of patriotism.

CHAPTER 13

Finally, the violent history of our world as it has played out in the passionate differences of religious beliefs, continues to this day in the bombing of abortion clinics and the vicious name calling that takes place in the halls of our government. The story of my life would not be complete without a discussion of my strong commitment to the separation of church and state. For some time now, there has been a concerted effort by some religious conservatives to enshrine their own religious doctrine into federal law. This is the model of many Arab states, such as Saudi Arabia where the civil law and religious law are one and the same.

When the colonists broke away from England it was, in part, to divorce themselves from the Church of England, because they resented having just one set of religious doctrine available to them. If we now allow religious doctrine to become federal law, or even state law, we return to our earlier condition, that is, we have only one set of religious doctrine available to us. The difference is that the earlier condition was imposed by the Church of England, while today it is being imposed by our State and Federal governments.

The funneling of tax dollars to religious schools, while public schools go without adequate funding, is a clear violation of the separation of church and state. Even if we had tons of money to throw around, which we don't, it would still be a violation of the separation of church and state. The idea of passing a federal law that would require prayer in public schools, or a law that would deny medical care to women who choose not to carry a fetus to term, is inconceivable to me. That puts us in the same category as those countries which have no civil law at all, they have only religious law. That is where we are headed if certain religious groups have their way.

This is difficult for me to believe, but some members of congress have been pushing a law that would make late term abortions illegal EVEN IF THE HEALTH, OR EVEN THE LIFE, OF THE MOTHER IS THREATENED. Men have treated women as subservient, without rights, for so long that they don't even realize that is what they are doing. And some women are so steeped in this kind of discrimination that they actually think it is acceptable, and support the male position. Personally, I have no idea whether abortion is a sin or not, but I do know that denying a woman the right to make her own decision about it is the worst kind of arrogance, as well as a denial of a woman's personal liberties. This kind of blatant discrimination should not be acceptable to any thinking person.

As for the argument that the only concern here is the "sanctity of life," that is laughable. The same people who deny a woman's rights based on the sanctity of life argument, yell loudly for the right to kill people who have been convicted of crimes.

In any case, the school prayer and abortion issues are religious issues and should be treated as such. Silent prayer is currently allowed in public schools under the law, and

it should be available to all children in
school. Why isn't it practiced? I believe it is
because the religious zealots want to
mandate verbal prayers, prayers spoken out
loud so the children will be taught what a
proper prayer sounds like. Of course, it will
sound just like the teacher's own prayers.
This is so transparent it is laughable. I would
also point out that spoken prayers can be
said at home any time. Children do not have
to learn how to pray in public school.

It seems like all the important issues that
people get all wild-eyed and emotional about
are somehow tied into religious beliefs. Since
there are few scientific facts related to religious
dogma, there appears to be a need to "prove"
beliefs by pushing everyone to accept them. I
suppose those who push their dogma feel that
if enough people hold the same beliefs, that
proves their validity. Unfortunately, it doesn't,
so we are doomed to forever listen to beliefs
presented as fact—beliefs presented to
Congress to pass into law—beliefs that fail to
make us feel closer to God, but do make us
fight the claim that others who believe
differently are going to burn in hell. All we
subversives can do is to keep fighting to

"render unto Caesar that which is Caesars, and unto God that which is God's." Prayer and sin belong in God's domain.

Even the protection of the environment (another issue near and dear to my heart) is a religious issue. There are two very different views of humankind's relationship to the environment. One view is based on Genesis 1:26 which reads, "And God said, Let us make man in our image, after our likeness; and let them have dominion over the fish of the sea, and over the fowl of the air, and over the cattle, and over all the earth, and over every creeping thing that creepeth upon the earth." Those who view this scripture as meaning that every creature is put on earth by God to serve man in whatever way man sees fit, are called dominionists. They believe that God did not intend us to worship nature and so we can do whatever we like with it—exploit it, use it up, or anything else we please. Pat Robertson, one of the founders of the Christian Coalition, defined that passage to mean that Christians should take dominion over all the major institutions and run them until Christ comes again. It is a view of the United States which would see the courts, legislatures, schools, and corporations all run by Christian believers. Certainly that is not what the framers of the Constitution had in mind.

The other view of nature comes from Genesis 2:15, which reads, "And the Lord God took the man, and put him in the garden of Eden to till it and to keep it." Those who follow this scripture believe this means that man is responsible for protecting the beauty of the earth and the other animals that live on it. This is called liberation theology. Those who subscribe to liberation theology view "dominion over the earth" to mean service and stewardship, and caring as modeled by Çhrist. They are concerned about such things as environmental pollution and the extinction of animal and plant species.

It is interesting to note that religious groups sometimes change their views of which of these interpretations is correct. In the process of doing research for my doctoral dissertation, I learned that there has been a shift in the Pentecostal movement from liberation theology (which emphasized such systemic problems as housing, human rights, unemployment, and racism) toward dominion theology. One Pentecostal minister characterized the schism in theological thought this way: "I was disillusioned to find that some believers in the movement that had been born in a stable were now being seduced by preachers who told them that God wanted them to have dominion over everything. I was infuriated by preachers who were telling trusting and vulnerable listeners that if they were poor or not in perfect health it was their own fault for not showing enough faith." If you are interested in learning more about dominion theology and liberation theology, you can read a book by H. Cox, titled *Fire from Heaven: The Rise of Pentecostal Spirituality and the Reshaping of Religion in the Twenty-first Century.*

My view of the separation of church and state also encompasses the political activities of churches, particularly the open support of political candidates. I had been hearing for several years that the conservative churches were endangering their tax-exempt status by advocating particular political candidates. Since the candidates they were supporting were not exactly the same as the candidates I supported, I decided to write my dissertation on "*An Analysis of the Relationship Between the Marketing Strategies Used by Protestant Churches in the United States, as Reflected in their Sermon Topics, and the Political Preferences of their Congregations.*" I wanted to find out if the sermons delivered in conservative churches really are different from those found in liberal churches. All the books I had read by religious scholars said there is a difference, but no one had actually polled Protestant ministers to find out.

I took the subjects that other scholars had agreed were "conservative" subjects along with those they agreed were "liberal" subjects, and I conducted a national survey of pastors to see if they were correct. The subjects listed were:

> The importance of prohibiting abortions;
>
> The importance of putting prayer back in the public schools;
>
> The importance of maintaining the separation of church and state;

The importance of fighting the homosexual agenda;

Protection of the civil rights of all, regardless of race, religion, or sexual preference;

Fighting for smaller government and lower taxes;

Taking a strong stand on environmental protection;

The importance of government providing financial aid to the poor;

Appropriate strategies for political activism to effect legislation;

The importance of being "born again."

I asked the pastors to rank those topics in order of the frequency with which they include them in their sermons. The results were interesting.

There were six topics the pastors specified in the top five preferences for sermons (to save space I will designate L for liberal and C for conservative):

The importance of prohibiting abortions: L=9.6%, C=45.2%

Appropriate Strategies for Political Action to Effect Legislation: L=45.4%, C=19.2%

The importance of being born again: L=53.35%, C=84.3%

Civil Rights for all regardless of Race, Religion, or Sexual Preference: L=81.8%, C=36.4%

Taking a strong Stand on Environmental Protection: L=53.3%, C=21.6%

As you can see, there definitely is a difference between the sermons in churches that are politically conservative and those that are politically liberal.

There was, however, one very big surprise. In the category of "appropriate strategies for political action to effect legislation", the liberals far outranked conservatives. This flew in the face of all the studies done by other authors on the matter of political activities in the churches. That seemed most peculiar to me, since other studies showed that conservative churches spend millions of dollars on voter guides to let their parishioners know how to vote. As far as I was able to discover in my research, for the most part this is a practice not employed by liberal churches. I have personally been in some conservative churches where I observed voter guides on display in the lobbies. Perhaps, I decided, the pastors in my survey were worried about jeopardizing their tax-exempt status so they decided to keep mum.

I wish there were time and money to do another survey, but alas, the question will have to remain unanswered. It is difficult to imagine, having heard pastors such as Pat Robertson and Jerry Falwell wax eloquent on the evils of liberal politicians, that they never mention any ways to effect legislation in their sermons.

This is still a very troublesome area to me. Some politicians hide their real agenda until after they are elected, then the truth emerges. Unfortunately, the American people are busy with their own lives and they don't watch what their representatives in government are voting for. Perhaps we subversives can overthrow apathy among American voters and non-voters. Perhaps as a people we can demand that our political representatives be truthful about what their values are—what their intentions are for their term of service, after they are elected to office. Certainly we are capable of that. Will we? Probably not. My mother once said to me, "I don't pay any attention to what is happening in the government—that is what I have elected representatives for." That probably represents the views of most Americans. I wish I could think like that—I would certainly sleep better.

Another very interesting piece of history emerged during my dissertation research. While Americans appear to be interested in the political thinking of our founders in the 18th century, there is not agreement as to exactly what the political philosophy of that